ALMA LAVENSON:

Wildwood Arts, Berkeley, California

PHOTOGRAPHS

Susan Ehrens

(Front Cover) Self-Portrait, 1932. Alma Lavenson

(Page i) Alma Lavenson, c. 1923. Photographer unknown

(Overleaf) Carquinez Bridge, 1933. Alma Lavenson

Quotations by Alma Lavenson
Pictorialism: Alma Lavenson (AL) interview with the
author (SE), 1986, transcript, p. 14.
Modernism: AL:SE, 1986, p. 15.
The Southwest: AL:SE, 1986, p. 24.
The Mother Lode and Virginia City [both quotes]:
Alma R. Lavenson, "Virginia City, Photographing a
'Ghost Town,'" *U.S. Camera Magazine,* Travel Section
no. 10, (June-July 1940), pp. 65,66.

First Edition. Printed in the United States of America.

ISBN 0-8263-1237-3 (Cloth)
ISBN 0-8263-1238-1 (Paper)

Library of Congress Catalog Card no. 90-071010

Wildwood Arts, P.O. Box 11426, Berkeley, CA 94704

Child with Doll, 1932. Alma Lavenson

Sweating Glass, 1931. Alma Lavenson

Contents

Acknowledgments

I want to express my deepest gratitude to Alma Lavenson's sons, Albert and Paul Wahrhaftig, and their wives, Madeline and Priscilla. This book would not have been realized without their encouragement and generous support.

Other family members and friends of Alma Lavenson provided valuable information and photographs. In particular, I am indebted to Jane Lukens for her perceptions, her sense of documentation, and her caring approach to this project, and to Joan Dunbar, who shared reminiscences with me and contributed research assistance at a time when it was especially appreciated. I also thank Rose-Etta Sampson and Jane Reber.

I am grateful to Susie Tompkins for her interest in Alma Lavenson and for her support of this project. I wish to acknowledge Merrily and Tony Page for their expert care in the preparation of the photographs for publication. Leonard and Marjorie Vernon, enthusiastic collectors of Alma Lavenson's photographs, generously made loans of the work for this book. I thank Raymond F. O'Brien for lending a photograph from The Consolidated Freightways, Inc. Collection, and Judy Kay and Anne Conway of Judy Kay and Associates, Inc., for facilitating the loan.

For permission to quote from Elinor Mandelson's extensive interview with Alma Lavenson, I thank Elinor Mandelson and Ruth Rafael, Archivist, Western Jewish History Center of the Judah L. Magnes Museum. I thank the people who offered advice and contributed assistance to this project: Mary Street Alinder; Abe Aronow; Dana Asbury, The University of New Mexico Press; John Collins; Bruce Dzieza; Ronald Sterling Egherman, The Friends of Photography; Neil A. Fiore; Christopher Forsyth; Paul M. Hertzmann; Therese Heyman, The Oakland Museum; Edwynn Houk; Michael Shapiro; Jean S. Tucker, The University of Missouri-St. Louis; Katherine Ware; and Reuben Weinzveg.

I especially want to thank four people who worked very closely with me on this book. Bruce Montgomery patiently and creatively embraced the challenges of this book to produce an elegant design. Gail Larrick, through her knowledge of photography and expertise as a perceptive editor, brought to the book an uncompromising clarity and objectivity. Her graciousness, humor, and sensitive insights into the material played a significant role in seeing this book to its fruition. Jay Fisher of The Baltimore Museum of Art was a supportive advisor and participant in the book's development. I am grateful for our many conversations, for his significant contribution to this publication, and for his friendship. I am deeply indebted to Leland Rice, who shared my friendship with Alma Lavenson during the last ten years of her life and was my partner in every aspect of this publication from its inception to on-press production. The time he devoted to this project was often at the expense of his own work. His curatorial capabilities are especially evident in the selection of photographs and refinement of the portfolio of Alma Lavenson's work.

I conclude with loving thoughts of Alma. I miss her. We began this project together, and I have felt her presence during this past year as I completed this book. I hope the presentation of her work is worthy of the quality and integrity she offered through her photography during her lifetime.

Susan Ehrens
September 1990

(*Right*) *Rowboats*, Lake Merritt, Oakland, 1929. Alma Lavenson

Alma Lavenson, 1926. Johan Hagemeyer

Alma Lavenson: An Enduring Vision

Alma Lavenson was eighty-two years old and had just begun her "second career in photography" when I first met her in 1979. With her practice of keeping detailed records of her exhibitions and publications, Alma had begun a new scrapbook that she called *After Eighty*, an affectionate reference to *After Ninety*, her friend Imogen Cunningham's final project. "I'm not going to wait that long," she told me. She was making new photographs and also reprinting some of her favorite images from the 1920s and 1930s.

I knew little of her first career, only that Alma, a self-taught amateur with rudimentary knowledge of photographic techniques, had been photographing for more than sixty years. Around 1918, she took up the camera as an amateur hobbyist; by the late 1920s, she was contributing frequently to pictorialist magazines and exhibiting regularly in national and international salons. During the early 1930s, Alma embraced the purist aesthetics now synonymous with Group f/64 and Precisionism, creating a body of work consistent in its quality and strength. In 1933, she was honored with one-person exhibitions of her photographs at the M. H. de Young Memorial Museum, San Francisco, and The Brooklyn Museum. She continued to participate in significant group exhibitions throughout the 1930s, 1940s, and 1950s, including *Family of Man*. She had one-person exhibitions at the San Francisco Museum of Modern Art in 1942, 1948, and 1960.

I worked with Alma Lavenson, and we became close friends. When she died in 1989, at the age of ninety-two, she left me to complete this book we had begun together. Only then did I begin to question the essential complexities of her ordered life. I began to wonder why Alma always insisted, "For me, photography was just a small part of my life," and why she consistently referred to herself as an amateur. As I studied Alma's photographs, I came to realize that only her view of herself as amateur separated her best work from that of her colleagues. As I made selections of her photographs and researched her life and exhibition history, I reflected on the vitality and integrity of her work. I came to appreciate that within the modest, almost self-effacing woman I knew, existed a power that Alma revealed most clearly in her photography.

Alma Lavenson, age nine, 1906.
Thors Studio, San Francisco

Alma Ruth Lavenson was born on May 20, 1897, the granddaughter of enterprising, Jewish immigrants from Europe who settled in the Mother Lode country of the untamed West during California's Gold Rush. She lived with her parents, Albert and Amy Lavenson, her maternal grandmother, and a bachelor uncle in a large sprawling Victorian in San Francisco. An only child, she was rarely alone, for aunts, uncles, and cousins lived nearby, and others visited regularly from North San Juan, California, her mother's birthplace. A strong sense of family nurturing shaped her happy, carefree childhood. At age eighty she recalled large family gatherings that she referred to fondly as "happy crowdings": "I can remember that my dream of the perfect way to live would be to have a long table with lots of children every night for dinner."

In 1906, San Francisco's great earthquake and fire caused Alma and her family to relocate across the Bay, to Oakland, where her father was vice president of the H. C. Capwell Company, one of the Bay Area's early department stores. When Alma was interviewed years later, she spoke often and with great affection about her father, who was clearly a significant influence on her life.

It is easy to see why Alma was so devoted to her father. Albert Lavenson was an innovative businessman, a generous philanthropist, and a highly respected community leader. He was well-known in the San Francisco Bay Area as "an enthusiastic booster for Oakland," which he firmly believed was a "city with a limitless future." Although he gave lavishly to his community and its cultural institutions, he was a modest man who lived quietly and moderately, focused upon family and friends. His greatest passion was music. He actively supported promising young musicians and helped build the music building at Mills College, Oakland, where, with his family, he rarely missed a concert.

Alma Lavenson's artistic character began to form quite naturally during her childhood, largely as a result of her father's arts and cultural interests and the social opportunities his position in the community afforded her. As a small child, she gravitated to him, sharing many of his interests and values. She took piano lessons and developed a love of music and travel akin to his. She inherited his modesty, quiet manners, and dry wit. Albert Lavenson has been described as a "quiet achiever," words that applied aptly to his daughter.

Alma Lavenson was graduated from the University of California, Berkeley, in 1919, with a degree in psychology. Following a seven-month Grand Tour of Europe with her parents, an aunt, and a cousin, Alma resumed piano lessons. She began to collect books and examples of fine printing, a lifelong interest that may have been influenced by her family's close friend, art patron and bibliophile Albert Bender. "He always managed to pass on what he thought would interest me," Alma told me, speaking often of and with great appreciation for Bender.

Alma also worked energetically as a volunteer in a number of community organizations. She felt great pride when she was offered a salaried position for her work at the pediatric clinic of Oakland's Community Health Center but, at her father's insistence, she returned her monthly check. "My father had rather old-fashioned ideas about girls working, if they didn't have to," Alma recalled, many years later. "He felt in the first place that it was wrong to take a job from someone who needed it, and in the second place, he felt it was a reflection on his ability to support his family." Alma was born in an era that frowned upon women maintaining professional lives, and she lived in an affluent genteel society that expected young women to be educated and cultured—but not necessarily employed.

Her father's unwillingness to allow her to establish a profession left a void in Alma's life. She filled that void by energetically pursuing her interest in photography.

Alma Lavenson made her first serious photographs about 1923, at the age of twenty-six. Her decision to photograph more seriously began as a personal search, a need for the creative self-expression that had eluded her. She knew no other photographers, no schools of photography or camera clubs. What she lacked in knowledge she made up for with enthusiasm, self-confidence, and a sense of adventure. She learned to develop film and print photographs by watching a technician at Bowman's drugstore, Oakland, as he went through the process with a roll of her own

Still Life, c. 1930. Alma Lavenson

film. This "lesson" was the extent of her formal training in photography. She turned her outdoor childhood playhouse into a darkroom where she experimented with a variety of gelatin silver papers. Her family didn't particularly encourage her growing commitment to photography, but, she remembered, "They were willing to have me muddle around."

Alma found technical instruction and practical advice in the pages of *Photo-Era Magazine, The Camera,* and the leading photography magazine on the West Coast, *Camera Craft.* These publications became her primary source of photographic information and inspiration. After reading advertisements in the magazines, Lavenson purchased an Ensign Reflex camera but replaced its sharp-focus lens with a second-hand soft-focus Waterbury lens that rendered softly defined atmospheric images in the pictorialist style promoted by the periodicals. She also studied books on composition. Early on, this concentration on the formal aspects of design became an essential strength of her work.

With friends, Alma hiked around Marin County and made romantic images of the rolling hillsides that flanked Mount Tamalpais. But what interested her most were Lake Merritt and the Estuary in Oakland, at that time a major industrial port. Each Sunday morning, she went to the Estuary with two friends, an etcher and a painter. While they sketched, Alma photographed the industrial and architectural forms of tanks, ships, barges, and storage elevators. The subject of her work was, in fact, light: the play of light on water, against a wall, or on the metallic surface of an industrial form. She became absorbed in the process of picturemaking: "I remember, when I was first interested in photography, I'd go along driving or walking and was continually composing mental pictures of what I saw along the way...."

The periodicals to which Alma subscribed announced forthcoming salons and published exhibition reviews illustrated with photographs that had received recognition. The magazines sponsored monthly photographic competitions and then, in the following issue, published the award-winning images with accompanying critiques. In 1927, Alma Lavenson sent her first submission, *The Light Beyond,* made in Zion National Park, Utah, to *Photo-Era Magazine.* To her surprise, the photograph was featured as the front cover and frontispiece of the December issue. This success encouraged her. It was her first recognition outside her family. Alma's

Pipeline, Oakland Estuary, 1926. Alma Lavenson

subsequent entries were praised by the editors as "strong in composition and atmosphere." They further remarked on her "thorough knowledge of effective lighting." Her photographic career was off to a promising start. During the next five years, Alma's photographs were frequently selected for publication, and she actively exhibited in national and international pictorialist salons.

The turning point in Alma's development as an artist came in 1930, coinciding with the death of her father. Albert Bender, who had encouraged her to purchase work from Diego Rivera during her 1926 Mexican journey, gave her letters of introduction to three photographers: Imogen Cunningham, Consuelo Kanaga, and Edward Weston. Alma's meetings with the three changed the course of her photographic career. Bender was actively interested in the work of the three photographers, and he was known to encourage and support young artists. He may have expected that Alma, in the philanthropic tradition of her father, would lend financial support to these photographers. He could not have known that within two years she would be one of the few invited to exhibit with them in the inaugural exhibition of the newly formed Group f/64.

Shyly, and with great hesitation, she telephoned Imogen Cunningham, who casually invited Alma to her home for a gathering. The two women became friends and remained close until Cunningham's death in 1976. "She was the greatest influence on anything that I have accomplished," Alma would say. She spoke to me often about their friendship and Cunningham's encouragement of her photography.

Alma took the letter of introduction from Albert Bender and her photographs to photographer Edward Weston during a trip to Carmel. She was reticent about asking for his advice. Weston was "a very gentle, likeable person who took a great interest in my work and in criticizing it," she recalled. He was "flattering about the composition—the way I saw things—but he objected to the pictorial approach." Alma disagreed with him and she boldly defended her "fuzzy lens." Later, possibly further convinced by Imogen Cunningham, Alma decided that Weston was right, and she retrieved the sharp-focus lens that came with her camera.

Alma made a seemingly effortless and rapid adjustment to sharp-focus:

Imogen Cunningham, Alma Lavenson, and Consuelo Kanaga, 1952. Alma Lavenson

"My work became clearer and straighter, less romantic," she said. Alma recognized the camera's inherent ability to flatten space and transform objects into abstract shapes. Industrial subjects became studies in the formal arrangements of light and dark, punctuated abstractly by sunlight and shadow. She composed her photographs simply and directly, capturing a distinctly modernist vision.

Despite the initial influence of Cunningham and Weston, Alma maintained a remarkable degree of independence in her photography. Among West Coast photographers, with the exception, perhaps, of Sonya Noskowiak, she was unique in her concentration on industrial and architectural themes. These subjects were traditionally favored by men, and they were often portrayed as symbols of the modern machine age. Alma's interest in machines was strictly formal. "I never took them as machinery. I always saw them as a composition of some sort," she said. Architectural and industrial forms were her primary subjects and straight photography her chosen aesthetic. Although her photographs span more than sixty years, her subjects and aesthetic were arrived at during the late 1920s, and her vision remained consistent.

Iris, 1932. Alma Lavenson

In 1932 Alma participated in a number of group exhibitions at the M. H. de Young Memorial Museum, with those photographers whose work she so respected. These included the international exhibition *Showing of Hands,* the landmark exhibition *Group f/64,* and the *California Trees* exhibition and competition, for which Alma Lavenson was awarded second prize, Edward Weston, first, and Ansel Adams, fourth. These exhibitions and others marked the end of her "salon period" and reinforced her position as a committed and accomplished photographer.

The following year Alma Lavenson was honored with one-person exhibitions at The Brooklyn Museum and at the de Young. The de Young exhibition included more than sixty photographs of plants and industrial studies, praised for their "high degree of technical excellence." The *San Francisco Chronicle* commented:

Miss Lavenson's choice of subject combines the pictorial with the more modern types, in which latter are seen smoke stacks, details of dry wood, and other objects selected for the display of pattern and texture. In her choice of papers for her prints she uses in each case the one that is best adapted to the subject and its textures....

This concentrated period of creativity and prolific exhibition work lasted through 1933. In September of that year Alma Lavenson married a brilliant attorney, Matt Wahrhaftig. She had known him for fourteen years. They had two sons: Albert, in 1935, and Paul, in 1938. Her family became her first priority and the subjects for much of her camera work. "Photography is my avocation," Alma explained bluntly. "My real full-time job is the care and training of two small boys and a husband." Never again would she enjoy a period so singularly devoted to creative camera work and exhibition activity.

Around 1933, Alma Lavenson began to photograph California's rapidly disappearing gold mining towns in the Sierra foothill region known as the Mother Lode. This interest developed when she visited her mother's birthplace, North San Juan. As she photographed churches, shops, signs, and walls, she felt the spirit of the place and of the past— of the California of her ancestors, of those who had mined for gold. She found deep personal meaning in her new subject and approached it with the dedication of an anthropologist. Her husband, Matt, the son of California immigrants, was deeply interested in history and became involved in his wife's project. "This is not a history of the Gold Rush, nor is it a complete photographic record of it," he wrote in 1948, in an introduction for a proposed book of Alma's Mother Lode photographs. "It is an attempt to reconstruct through the medium of the camera the spirit of a period rather than a literal record of it…." Alma carefully studied maps and histories of the Mother Lode, and organized her photographs and negatives alphabetically by town. "Californians still love those names —and well they should. For where else would one find Rough and Ready, Red Dog or You Bet?" Matt asked in his introduction. "Where else would Whiskey Slide thrive, a neighbor to Jesus Maria? Who but the boisterous, footloose goldseekers would have called their settlements Hangtown or Poker Flat or Fiddletown?"

Alma created a compellingly accurate record of these towns. Still, she did not consider herself a documentary photographer. She was interested in the formal qualities of her subjects and sought to capture them with the objectivity of her industrial studies. In 1948, Alma's Mother Lode photographs were featured in her second one-person exhibition at the San Francisco Museum of Modern Art. Alfred Frankenstein, art critic

El Dorado, 1949. Alma Lavenson

Spiral, Tomar, Portugal, 1962. Alma Lavenson

for the *San Francisco Chronicle,* praised the work:

…she has simply set up her camera before the streets and houses of those old California towns and taken some of the most perfect photographs of them in the history of camera work. They are remarkable not only for detail, their formal perception, and their atmospheric qualities; over and above this they have a luster, variety, and depth that are almost unparalleled in photography.

Alma tried unsuccessfully in 1947 and again in 1979 to realize publication of a book of her Mother Lode photographs. After Matt's death in 1957, the project became not only a spiritual remembrance of her grandparents and her mother but a loving homage to her husband. Her book was never published.

For about ten years, beginning in the late 1960s, Alma Lavenson made very few photographs, except during her travels to foreign countries. "I felt out of step with the trend to far out and experimental photography which was being accepted and exhibited," she explained. "I am still a straight photographer." She was referring to the use of the camera by many contemporary photographers to express the subjective, the psychological, and the mystical—realms that she did not embrace in her photography. The purist aesthetics championed by Group f/64, it seemed, were out of fashion.

For many years, Alma Lavenson's photographs were unknown to photography curators, to historians, and to the public. Two things changed that and precipitated her "second career." In 1978, Jean Tucker, of the University of Missouri-St. Louis, organized a traveling exhibition to recreate the 1932 Group f/64 exhibition. This exhibit caused a renewed historic and aesthetic interest in the work of Alma Lavenson. The following year, the California Museum of Photography, Riverside, California, organized Alma's first retrospective exhibition, accompanied by a catalog. "Always very discriminating in her subject matter and selective in what she exhibited, Lavenson has a secure reputation, soundly established on the high quality of her work," Louis William Fox wrote in *Artweek,* reviewing the Riverside exhibition. Alma's work, largely unfamiliar to a new but appreciative audience, was widely praised. With renewed enthusiasm, she began photographing again. Her earlier interest in architectural and industrial forms, especially tanks, was rekindled.

"I like to photograph industrial things and I used to do that at the Oakland Estuary," she told an interviewer. "There were no fences then. Now everything has a high fence and a guard."

At times Alma seemed surprised at being rediscovered. Despite her modest manners, she may have expected to be granted such recognition. She was not self-promoting, and she did not sell her work even when, during the 1970s, a market materialized for photography. Clearly the social pressures that prevented her from seeking monetary compensation for her work had caused Alma to consider her photography—in fact, all the work she did—as an avocation. Yet for some sixty years she had documented her photographic prints and negatives and filed them with care. Her meticulous exhibition and publication records and the extensive activity they revealed belied the casual attitude she expressed toward her work. Alma had kept all her photographs, intending someday to donate them to a museum. But in 1983, she decided to sell her work. Her photographs were purchased by a number of museums and private collectors. Alma Lavenson's photographs have subsequently been included in significant exhibitions and publications focusing on the modernist vision of photography between the two world wars, and celebrating important camerawork by woman photographers.

Alma Lavenson may not have regarded photography as her profession, but it was certainly her life's major preoccupation. In 1986, at the age of eighty-nine, she gave up her volunteer work to devote more time to photography. "I've retired from everything except my interest in life and what I can still do in photography," she told an interviewer. In the final years of her life, the importance her photography held for her grew clear to both of us. During those years, Alma Lavenson emerged for me as a woman of great integrity, strength, and inner motivation, who captured the essence of her subjects. I came to understand that the modernist vision she embraced in her photographs was the perfect aesthetic for this woman who was grounded in logic and reality. The structural logic of her photographs and her life were one.

Susan Ehrens

Notes

With her practice of keeping: Alma Lavenson (AL) interview with Elinor Mandelson, September 25, 1978–April 21, 1980, transcript, p. 67. The Oral History Collection, Western Jewish History Center, Judah L. Magnes Museum. Hereafter called "AL:EM."

"For me, photography…": AL correspondence with Jean Tucker, October 1, 1977.

"happy crowdings": Jane Lukens, telephone conversation with the author, May 3, 1990.

"I can remember that my dream…": AL:EM, p. 5.

He was well-known: Ibid., p. 59-64. Also, newspapers clippings about Albert Lavenson in Alma Lavenson Wahrhaftig Family Collection (ALWFC).

Albert Lavenson has been described: Alan Furth, telephone conversation with the author, May 29, 1990.

"He always managed to pass…": AL interview with the author, 1986, transcript, p. 22. Hereafter called "AL:SE"

"My father had rather old-fashioned…": AL:EM, p. 46.

"They were willing to have me muddle…": AL:SE, p. 6.

"I remember, when I was first interested…": AL:EM, p. 56.

Alma's subsequent entries were praised: Photo-Era Magazine, Vol. 62, no. 5 (May 1929), p. 271; Vol. 63, no. 2 (August 1929), p. 100.

"She was the greatest influence…": AL:SE, p. 2.

Weston was "a very gentle, likeable…": Ibid., p. 3.

"My work became clearer…": Ibid.

"I never took them as machinery…": Ibid., p. 15.

"Miss Lavenson's choice of subject…": San Francisco Chronicle, April 16, 1933. Newspaper clipping, n.p., n.d., ALWFC.

"Photography is my avocation…": Alma R. Lavenson, "Virginia City: Photographing a 'Ghost Town,'" U.S. Camera 1943. New York: Duell, Sloan & Pierce, 1943, p. 101.

"This is not a history of the Gold Rush…": Matt Wahrhaftig, p. 4. Unpublished essay, dated 1948, ALWFC.

"Californians still love those names…": Ibid., p. 2.

"She has simply set up her camera…": Alfred Frankenstein, San Francisco Chronicle, August 8, 1948, p. 21. Newspaper clipping, ALWFC.

"I felt out of step…": Alma Lavenson correspondence with Jean Tucker, October 1, 1977.

"Always very discriminating…": Louis William Fox, "Alma Lavenson—The Spirit of Place," Artweek, Vol. 10, no. 7 (February 19, 1979), p. 11.

"I like to photograph…": Nancy Kieffer, "Her talent comes to light: Recognition gaining on photographer Alma Lavenson," The Montclarion, August 26, 1986, p. 11.

"I've retired from everything except…": Ibid.

Zion Canyon (The Light Beyond), 1927. Alma Lavenson

Resonant Light:
A Path to
Modernism

The perfect balance of lines, afforded by the opposing angles of the cliffs, has been made good use of by the artist, who knew just what she wanted and how to obtain it…. The sense of atmosphere is exquisite and is enhanced by the dreamy diaphanous cloud, drifting through the canyon. Surely a lovely picture; and as this is Miss Lavenson's initiatory effort in Photo-Era *competition, we hope to see more of her work.*

—Photo-Era Magazine, *December 1927*

Aside from the flowery prose, with its delight in atmosphere and the passing of a "diaphanous" cloud, this anonymous critique of Alma Lavenson's first published photograph, quintessentially pictorialist, could just as well have been written about her modernistic/precisionist pictures of the 1930s, resonating as they do with a pure, formalist vision. The qualities that caused Lavenson's pictorial photographs to receive awards in the international pictorialist salons of the late 1920s transcended mere technique and were swiftly recognized by the members of Group f/64, who invited her to participate in their first group exhibition in 1932.

Whether her images were soft or sharp in focus, Lavenson's photographic vision is remarkably consistent. Her choice of landscapes and occasional portraits, romantic in sentiment but composed with a formalist's eye, evolved to an equally contemplative study of man-made forms. Even in her pictorial work, she rarely photographed people, choosing to avoid the pastoral narratives so common to pictorialism. Clearly this self-confident, unassuming artist was most comfortable with the private photographic study of still life, whether composed with pieces of glass on a table or with dark shapes of industrial machinery flattened against the gleaming, convex skin of a metal storage tank, each rivet revealed in clear focus.

Alma Lavenson was born in San Francisco in 1897. She had the good fortune to live in an area that became, in the period of her artistic maturity, a most vital artistic community for the growth of photography. Having finished her psychology studies at the University of California several years before, Lavenson developed an interest in photography about 1923. In the absence of any formal artistic training or technical courses in photography, her interest began as a hobby; she first made pictures of friends and family. She learned to develop and print film, secured her own darkroom, and avidly read photographic magazines such as *Camera Craft*, a San Francisco magazine, *The Camera*, or *Photo-Era Magazine* that advocated pictorialism. Soon her folding Kodak camera was inadequate to the task. She acquired an English 3¼ x 4¼-inch reflex camera, put away its sharp-focus lens, and chose instead a Waterbury uncorrected lens, which achieved the fuzzy atmospheric look prescribed by these pictorialist publications.

In the company of friends, Lavenson photographed the hilly landscape of the San Francisco Bay Area as well as the industrial sites in and around the Oakland estuary. Her first entry in the frequent competitions championed by the publications she read was *The Light Beyond* (now titled *Zion Canyon*), taken on a family trip to Utah. Its subsequent appearance as the award-winning cover of *Photo-Era Magazine* encouraged in this beginner even more work and many additional submissions to publications and exhibitions in this country and Europe. Her efforts at publication met with great success.

After her father's death in 1930, Lavenson spoke with long-time family friend Albert Bender, a well-known philanthropist and a tireless supporter of the Bay Area arts community. He encouraged her to meet other photographers working in the area and gave her letters of introduction to Imogen Cunningham, Consuelo Kanaga, and Edward Weston. Lavenson visited Cunningham first, having recently acquired as her first photographic purchase Cunningham's *Magnolia Blossom*. This meeting began a lifelong friendship that would have a major influence on Lavenson's work as a photographer.

Not long after their meeting, and with Cunningham's encouragement, Lavenson visited Edward Weston. As Weston wrote later in his daybook, she invited criticism but fought his suggestions. He had admired

Masts and Funnels, 1930. Alma Lavenson

the abstract conception of *Masts and Funnels* (1930) but decried the soft focus, so inconsistent with its more radical composition. According to Lavenson's memories of their meeting, Weston suggested that concrete objects should be photographed in a concrete way. Her contact with Weston and undoubtedly the influence of Cunningham and Kanaga led Lavenson to abandon the Waterbury lens and revert to the original sharp-focus lens. Weston and Cunningham were no doubt less interested in obtaining a convert to "straight" photography than in encouraging the purist vision they saw behind the generalizing light of Lavenson's pictorialist style. For Lavenson it must have been an instinctive adjustment; she began immediately to take photographs that fully realized her innately formalist vision.

Lavenson continued to submit her earlier pictorialist photographs for exhibition and publication even while she was pursuing the new orientation. In a photographic world still dominated by the pictorial style, her new straight work, it was evident, would not have garnered the same admiration. A growing acceptance of straight photography was becoming evident in the magazines to which she submitted her work, however, and by 1931 her photograph *Composition in Glass* was both selected for publication in *Camera Craft* and accepted in the Chicago Salon. Soon after, her new work gained wide acceptance in other salons and publications. In addition to *Composition*, several plant studies were her most common submissions. An October 1931 entry in the *Irish Salon of Photography* appears to be Lavenson's last major submission of pictorial photographs. By 1933, Lavenson chose to eliminate her pictorial images from the several one-person exhibitions she had that year.

Pictorialism must have had the same value for Lavenson as it had for most straight photographers working in this era, including Alfred Stieglitz and Weston, among others. As a style, pictorialism argued persuasively for the photograph's artistic equality with painting and fostered a serious aesthetic orientation for those who practiced it. Two images—one pictorialist, *Sunlit Wheels* (1929), and one purist, *Glass Studies* (1931)—provide an excellent illustration of the transformation evident in Lavenson's photography during these years. *Sunlit Wheels* is a shallow view of a large spoked wheel; in front, a small pushcart is supported by an oversized wheel similar in construction to the other. This view, so compact and without depth, eliminates the suggestion of real interior space. We

Composition in Glass, 1931. Alma Lavenson

do not know the size or character of the surroundings. Surfaces and details are generalized by the diffuse focus, but Lavenson is careful not to conceal the solidity and structure of the objects in the imprecise focus of her pictorialist lens nor to lose the structured character of her composition in the prominent overlay of glaring highlights. Her attention to form and structure links her early work with that of other photographers such as Weston and Charles Sheeler who abandoned pictorialism for the precisionist orientation. The photograph is made eloquent through its quiet concentration and the visual control of a few carefully chosen compositional elements.

In *Glass Studies*, a variation of the photograph Lavenson exhibited in 1931, the diffuse light and imprecise realization of detail are replaced by the keen focus of a new approach. Glass containers are arranged one inside the other in decreasing sizes; they are placed on a table made shallow by foreground cropping. An indistinct background, probably a window with a blurred view, is too distant for recognition. A single container, one of the smallest in the group, is placed slightly forward and to the side. The repetition of form in the containers is highlighted through a succession of glaring reflections, at once revealing of both the surface and transparency of the containers. It is a photograph composed in the studio, analytical and striving for objectivity without pictorial narrative: form studied with light in shallow space. Only the technique has changed. For Lavenson, the change must have been a revelation.

These new purist photographs garnered continuing praise for Lavenson in the international salons but particularly in San Francisco at a number of exhibitions at the M. H. de Young Memorial Museum. Most notable was a 1932 exhibition, *Showing of Hands*, limited to the study of hands, where Lavenson, Cunningham, Weston, and others contributed photographs made especially for the occasion. These photographs are Lavenson's only studies of the human body; she never photographed a nude. The assignment was an interesting challenge to her developing purist vision, and she approached it with typical concentration and imagination. *Hands of the Etcher* and *Child with Doll*, both from 1932, show hands posed but natural in shallow space, composed in isolation from the rest of the figure. The viewer is given the barest of details, sufficient only to establish a thematic context: the top of an etching press, or the child's mouth and nose. In *Child with Doll*, Lavenson is careful to avoid showing the whole face, eyes, or facial expression, so that she can avoid the distracting sentimentality this image could easily convey. The etcher's hands soiled from work come closest to suggesting a narrative, but even in this image Lavenson's frozen study of form is timeless. Nothing extraneous compromises her concentration on detail and her fascination with form. What makes these works poignantly unexpected is the fact that Lavenson did not view these hands as inanimate objects in an arranged still life. The photographs breathe life, revealing the artist's human understanding and a deep respect for the associative and formal qualities of this most expressive of human features.

These new photographs, often exhibited with those of other purist photographers in the San Francisco Bay Area, were certainly noticed by artists and critics alike. In November 1932, Lavenson was invited, with Preston Holder, Consuelo Kanaga, and Brett Weston, to participate in the first exhibition of Group f/64 at the de Young. While Group f/64 did mount another exhibition before disbanding in 1935, the de Young show was the only major museum exhibition the group was granted. Included in Group f/64 were Ansel Adams, Imogen Cunningham, John Paul Edwards, Sonya Noskowiak, Henry Swift, Willard Van Dyke, and Edward Weston. Lavenson was suggested to the group by Cunningham; her work was well-known to the others, including Weston, who had noticed that she "had seen the light."

The nontheoretical Lavenson must have been pleased with the decidedly informal, nondoctrinaire spirit that linked the artists of Group f/64. In the following years she exhibited frequently with other members of Group f/64 and was given a one-person show at Willard Van Dyke's 683 Brockhurst gallery in 1934. Lloyd Rollins, then director of the de Young, was a major catalyst in gaining public exposure for these photographers. His efforts included the endorsement of both the group show and of Lavenson's one-person show at the de Young in April 1933. His subsequent departure from the de Young Museum brought to an end that institution's active role in exhibiting contemporary photography, a role that gradually shifted to the San Francisco Museum of Art.

While Lavenson exhibited with members of the short-lived Group f/64, she was not actually a member of the small group. She admitted that she sometimes felt uncomfortable in the company of Group f/64 mem-

Hands of an Etcher (Harry Schary), 1932. Alma Lavenson

bers because, unlike them, she did not devote her entire life to photography. Writing in 1973, San Francisco Museum of Art Curator John Humphrey, in an article describing the Swift Collection at the museum, made the mistake of diminishing Lavenson's importance because of her part-time status: "The recent additions were, for the most part, however, curious amateurs like Alma Lavenson, attracted more by the dynamic personalities than by serious commitments to a personal expression and photographic form." This short-sighted view could not be further from the truth. The comment reflects a prejudice that is often articulated to dismiss the part-time artist or amateur rather than coming to terms with the art itself. This far-too-common view has, until recently, inhibited a proper analysis of Lavenson's contributions.

Lavenson's conversion to straight photography after her conversation with Weston in 1930 stimulated a period of tremendous productivity that extended through the Group f/64 exhibition in 1932 and reached its height with her one-person exhibition at the de Young in 1933. In two photographs of 1931, *Tank* (included in the Group f/64 exhibition) and *Calaveras Dam*, the character of Lavenson's photographic vision can be defined. The two photographs differ in conception: *Tank* provides a detached study of abstraction, while the pyramidlike *Dam* is studied romantically with a dramatic realization of the contrasts of light and shadow. Light is central to both images. The tank is studied in full illumination that transforms its rounded superstructure to a flattened fabric of interwoven lines. For the dam, Lavenson uses highlights to pick out from the dark shadow that enshrouds the face of the dam its step-by-step structure. Rarely is deep space apparent in Lavenson's photographs. The subject is cropped, eliminating horizon lines and removing any wider context that might distract from the concentrated analysis of a structure's formal qualities. The photographer almost always chooses an unexpected point of view, often at an acute angle to the conventional straight-on shot that would have recorded mere appearance.

In their photographs of steel manufacturing plants, Charles Sheeler and Edward Weston explored the precision of industrial shapes with a clear interest in scale and monumentality in addition to formal abstraction. Lavenson's closeup views are more like miniatures. They are compact, exquisitely realized, and inclusive, while Sheeler's photographs of the River Rouge plant, for instance, extend outward, acknowledging scale and the dynamics of the industrial activity. Lavenson's studies of form are more immediate and contemplative. *Carquinez Bridge* (1933) is dissected and cropped so that we experience the abstract patterns of the bridge's metal superstructure rather than the immensity of its scale in relation to cars or the surrounding landscape. Another striking photograph of 1933, *Calaveras Cement Works*, show a consummate balance between attention to minute detail and large shapes, both studied by way of light and shadow. One feels that these photographs make visual a private world and that the photographer used what was accessible. In accord with her personality, Lavenson would have been unlikely to ask special permission for privileged access to restricted sites nor would she have used possibly dangerous vantage points. Her photography reveals self-reliance, modesty of purpose, and a pure concentration on ideas, apart from temporal concerns.

A group of plant studies made in 1931, including *Calla Leaf* and *Chrysanthemum*, immediately suggests the influence of Cunningham and establishes an interesting departure from the industrial scenes more common to Lavenson's work of this period. The sensibility of these photographs is close to that of the hand studies, also from 1931. While Cunningham and Lavenson shared a common subject, the difference in their approaches clearly indicates their individual styles. When Cunningham viewed a plant form, she was always fascinated with its sculptural, three-dimensional form. Her subject is the wholeness of a plant form. Light both penetrates the form and reflects its surface in studies that are sensuous and full of outward feeling.

Chrysanthemum, 1931. Alma Lavenson

The intimacy and open sexuality of Cunningham's plant studies contrast with Lavenson's more detached works. Lavenson is engaged instead by the plant's surface, patterns, and shapes and by a play of light that often creates its own formal reality. The photographs do not exhibit the pictorial depth of Cunningham's. Plants are analyzed for their potential as flattened abstract forms. They suggest a process of dissection and synthesis rather than a subjective realization of natural form.

In 1933, the year of her exhibition at the de Young Museum and her marriage to Matt Wahrhaftig, she began a body of work that occupied her for many years: photographs of the California gold country in the Sierra foothills, known as the Mother Lode. By 1935, when Group f/64 disbanded and Edward Weston and Willard Van Dyke left the San Francisco Bay Area, this project and additional work undertaken during travel with her husband replaced the more analytical, purist images familiar in earlier years. This is not to say that her new place-oriented views of the Mother Lode depart from the basic tenets of the Group f/64 approach, for they retain the same visual orientation with studied compositions and a keen focus on form revealed with the ever-present study of light.

The maturity of her photographic vision and unrelenting commitment to the art of photography did not lead Lavenson to an ambitious search for public recognition in these years. In 1933, she did exhibit a retrospective selection of her photographs in a one-person show at the Brooklyn Institute of Arts and Sciences (now the Brooklyn Museum) in New York, the only time her work would be shown in the East until her 1988 exhibition in Baltimore. Unfortunately we know little about the circumstances of the 1933 exhibition, and few critical reactions have been recorded. In 1937, while traveling in the East, she did, at Cunningham's insistence, make the required pilgrimage to Stieglitz's gallery, An American Place, but the visit affected her little. Stieglitz apparently gave her one of his legendary brushoffs, but far from being discouraged in the pursuit of her photography, Lavenson simply found him disagreeable.

Regrettably it is difficult to construct a comprehensive critical record of Lavenson's work in the years after 1937, as there was little published reaction to either her group or one-person shows. Lavenson's own notebooks provide a record of an active schedule of exhibitions. These notebooks reveal that as Lavenson's concentration on the Mother Lode work became exclusive, she rarely exhibited her earlier work, whether pictorialist or purist. Not until 1966, with a renewed interest in Group f/64 and the photography of the 1940s, was her pre-Mother Lode work exhibited again. This encouraged a worthwhile reconsideration and integrated study of her work in conjunction with better-known contemporaries. The Group f/64 exhibition in Oakland in 1966 and the St. Louis recreation of the original show in 1978 reestablished the historical context for Lavenson's photographs.

Most important was a timely exhibition, *Images of America: Precisionist Paintings and Modern Photography*, organized at the San Francisco

Museum of Art, which illustrated Lavenson's precisionist authority. Her transition from pictorialism to the purism of the late 1930s was the subject of the Baltimore exhibition. Her photographs are now widely collected by museums and private collectors who seek a broader representation of this crucial epoch in the history of photography, and who recognize the merits of Alma Lavenson's artistic contribution.

Jay McKean Fisher
Curator of Prints, Drawings, and Photographs
The Baltimore Museum of Art

(Right) Calla Leaf, 1931. Alma Lavenson

Pictorialism

One of my earliest interests in photography was industrial because the Oakland waterfront was fascinating and full of activity. The Alaskan fishing fleet used to come down and anchor in the Estuary over the winters with their sails and masts…

Sunday on the Estuary, Oakland, 1926

Alaskan Fishing Fleet, Oakland Estuary, 1926

Grain Elevator, 1929

Anchored Rowboats, 1929

Waterfront, 1929

Sunlit Wheels, 1929

Dredger, 1929

Danse Macabre, 1930

Iron Balcony, 1929

Modernism

The industrial subjects lent themselves to a pure vision. I began to photograph from a closer vantage point, emphasizing the forms and texture, strong sunlight and shadows, across the tanks, ships, and dams.

Locomotive, 1930

Standard Oil Tanks, 1931

Pole and Shadow, c. 1929

Silhouette of a Tank, 1933

Calaveras Cement Works, 1933

Union Oil Tanks, Alameda, 1931

Calaveras Dam II, 1932

Tank, 1931

Egg Box, 1931

Calaveras Cement Works II, 1933

Composition f/64, 1931

The Southwest

*I was intensely interested in lifestyles
different from ours, and this was the
beginning of a long series of trips to
various civilizations and other countries.
I was interested in compositions—as
I had always been—and forms and deep
shadows created by bright sunlight.*

Entrance to Kiva, Frijoles Canyon, New Mexico, 1928

Indian Ovens II, New Mexico, 1941

Girl Winnowing I, New Mexico, 1928

Girl Winnowing II, New Mexico, 1928

Ancient Community Dwellings, Frijoles Canyon, New Mexico, 1941

Cliff Dwellings, Mesa Verde National Park, Colorado, 1941

Church, Las Trampas, New Mexico, 1941

Church, Las Trampas, New Mexico, 1941

Church, Las Trampas, New Mexico, 1941

Entrance to Church, Ranchos de Taos, New Mexico, 1941

Gathering Storm II, New Mexico, 1941

Clouds, New Mexico, 1941

St. Charles Hotel, Downieville, 1934

Pump and Trough, Hornitos, 1940

Robert Bell's Store, Coloma, 1946

66

Barn, North Bloomfield, Nevada City, 1938

Jail, Coloma, 1947

Bear Valley, 1947

I wanted to catch the spirit of the town—the intense deep blue of the sky with its fantastic clouds, the arid desert atmosphere, the rakish old buildings with their gaudy pasts, the dusty roads and crazily crooked wooden sidewalks. Often I waited seemingly endless time for automobiles or present-day residents in modern dress to move out of the scene. I hoped that the spirits of the old-timers of bygone days would fill the streets instead.

View from Above with Church, Virginia City, 1939

Court House, Virginia City, 1943

"Food Products," Virginia City, 1939

Firehouse, The Divide, Virginia City, 1939

Ruined Building, Virginia City, 1943

Church, Chinese Camp, 1939

Untitled, Cholula. Alma Lavenson

(Overleaf) Untitled, On the road to Cacahuamilpa. Alma Lavenson

Old Mexico: Travel Letters 1926

*A*lma Lavenson's Mexican travel journal was drawn from letters to her family. She traveled with a friend, Phyllis, and Hattie, their informal chaperone. The accompanying Mexican photographs were discovered in Lavenson's darkroom shortly after her death.

Just Out of Juarez, March 7

Lookit! We're in Mexico!!…

This letter is being written very much in pieces, for every so often the scenery claims my attention. Sometimes it is rolling, smooth white sand dunes that only need a couple of camels and a sheik to make it look just like the Sahara. Sometimes it is a rugged blue or far-distant pink mountain, and sometimes a little cluster of square adobe huts out of which swarm an incredible number of women and children and dogs and pigs. At each of these little settlements the train stops for ages, just as though we had all the time in the world and weren't dying to really arrive someplace.…

We've just passed a fairly good sized little town with one main street and rows and rows of little adobe huts surrounding it. The train stopped long enough for me to snap a rather interesting adobe house with a wooden balcony running across the front. The whole population which was loafing about was much interested, and a machine full of Mexican cowboys carefully posed themselves, thinking they were the big attraction. They cheered us wildly as we pulled out.…

Luna Hotel, Guanajuato, March 10

Viva la Mexico! Our first day of adventure was such a complete and entire success that I've wakened at 6:30 this morning so I'll have plenty of time to tell you all about it.…

[After a visit to a nearby park and a drive with new friends found by the gregarious Hattie], the road home took us past a wide river bed (with very little river in it) where hundreds of *peones* were engaged in making adobe bricks. Women were washing clothes in what little muddy water there was, little groups of burros grazed on the scant tufts of grass. The houses along the river were flat, square affairs, and stone bridges, centuries old, spanned the river bed. Altogether it was the sort of scene we love to stop and gaze at, but as usual we were hastily whirled by it all and had to catch what fleeting glimpses we could as we flew along.…

Someday we are going to write a Guanajuato Symphony, for there was never a more musically noisy town than this. Beginning early in the morning and lasting till late at night (sometimes too late for us tired souls) the air is filled with the sound of church bells, the peddlers' musical calls, the braying of burros, the adorable soprano toot of the streetcar horns and the musical voices of the people. Occasionally at night, the twang of a guitar is added to the Symphony, with a few voices made more or less melodious by an evening at the neighboring cantina, harmonizing in the Mexican equivalent of "Sweet Adeline."… Then we drove to the Valenciana mine where we were…thrilled by the exquisite church which commands a hilltop near the mine, and by the gorgeously colorful views of the rugged mountains all about us, the vivid turquoise sky, and the clouds.…

Luna Hotel, Guanajuato, March 11

At 6:30 in the morning we rose with the church bells, and after a hasty breakfast cooked on my little sterno we sorrowfully said goodbye to our hotel and our beloved plaza.… The venders were spreading their wares out under their little canvas awnings, and a few early rising burros were beginning to make their appearance. It was all so lovely…and yet the people we meet on the trains or at the hotels simply can't understand what brings us to an old-fashioned place like Guanajuato. Why don't we go to Monterrey? that's a big city…much business…lots of industries…that's a beautiful place! But Guanajuato! Why, that's nothing at all!!

Guadalajara, March 13

Once more I am writing at 6:30 a.m., propped up in bed. I simply can't get used to sleeping through those energetic church bells which seem to be more than ever vociferous here.... The little towns that we pass on the train, and the busy scenes at the stations where we stop for a few minutes remind me of nothing so much as the opening scenes of most any comic opera, where the brilliantly dressed peasants wander back and forth on the stage with baskets and trays full of wares, singing and keeping the orchestra company until the prima donna appears....

Guadalajara, March 14

Once again it is 6:30 a.m. and I can't sleep. This time it is because I am dreadfully worried. It's time for the bells to begin and they haven't. Do you suppose the priest has overslept? And what happens to priests who oversleep and forget to ring their bells?...

Our chaperone [Hattie] has the most unique habit of suddenly disappearing completely as though she had gone up in smoke. Then Phyllis and I comb all the nearby doorways and eventually find her making herself perfectly at home in the least expected place. This time we got out of the machine to take a picture of a charming church.... When we returned, there was no Hattie.... In desperation we tooted and tooted...and finally she emerged from a house, followed by all the women of the household, and carrying a bunch of roses which they had taken her up on the roof to pick!...

Guadalajara, March 16

We had such a nice all-day auto trip yesterday to Lake Chapala.... We rode through gently rolling farm country.... Sometimes we passed oxen drawing clumsy two-wheeled wooden carts, and often we met little groups of burros laden with hay or wood or peat. Sometimes the loads are so enormous that they look like four-legged haystacks out for a walk....

We passed through the most primitive villages of little adobe huts with thatched roofs, and had a glorious time stopping every two minutes to take pictures. We lost Hattie twice, each time in a little village school, but as soon as we heard the children singing, we knew where she was and waited patiently for her to come out....

Untitled, Near Chapala. Alma Lavenson

Muchacho, Zapopan. Alma Lavenson

We hired a tiny motor boat and rowed about on the lake [Chapala] for a while. Then we stopped at a tiny island inhabited solely by two perfectly sweet fishermen, their pig and chickens and goats and fishing nets. They were…quite pleased to have their pictures taken, though one of them did insist on reading a newspaper as he posed, giving the picture quite a literary effect.…

After lunch we wandered along the bank a little, and then returned to Guadalajara, still enthusing about the landscape, and still hopping out every few minutes to take pictures.…

Hotel Mancera, Mexico City, March 18

After the very Mexican towns we have stopped in until now, we are having quite a time adjusting ourselves to Mexico City.… Although Guadalajara is the second largest city in the republic, it still has a sleepy, easy-going air to it and strangers are a rare enough sight to be stared at. Now we are in a big city which could be anywhere in Europe. The streets are filled with hurrying people of every nationality, you hear nearly as much English spoken as Spanish, and European hats and clothes have almost completely replaced the sombreros and serapes and sandals.…

We stopped to call on a couple of brothers named Loevy to whom Hattie had a letter.… They are a pair of bachelors and have stepped right out of a Dickens novel…both rather small and slightly shriveled and awfully polite.…

[In Zapopan] there came along the most adorable little urchin I've ever seen. He was about six years old, with a tangled mop of curly black hair, a chubby dirty face, the most lovable grin which revealed a couple of missing front teeth, a red shirt, and trousers which had once been white and may have once been whole, but were now a most complicated affair of rags and tatters. I simply had to have a picture of him, but the first time in our travels, a penny had absolutely no effect…he was afraid of the camera and he wouldn't pose. I offered him the tin foil from a roll of films, which usually captivates the youngsters here, but even that failed to move him. I went through an elaborate pantomime of taking Hattie's picture, just to show him how painless it all was, but still he refused. Even another penny left him cold, and at last, tired of our coaxing, he turned and scuttled down the street, disappearing among the little houses.… "Never mind," said Hattie. "I'll get him for you," and off she went in the direction where he had disappeared. She too vanished from sight, but only for a few minutes…then a small procession made its way up the street. First came Hattie, then a Mexican woman, who proved to be the small boy's mother, then his sister holding very securely onto the hand of our youngster who formed a very unwilling wind-up to the parade. It seems Hattie had wandered down the street, peeking into every doorway, until she finally discovered him, hiding under the family bed. She explained to his mother how much we admired her offspring, so with the aid of the muchly-flattered parent, the sister, the penny and the tin foil, we finally got the picture. The younster, finding that pictures don't really hurt after all, became quite radiant, our tardy street-car finally arrived, and like all good stories, it all ended very happily.

Mexico City, March 19

I don't know about that picture for Mills [College], Dad. We haven't had a chance to see any of [Diego] Rivera's work, and…I gather that he isn't half as well thought of here as in the States, and find it very difficult to get any information about him.… I have found out that the gentleman mostly does murals, and a mural is so hard to send home!

We were asked to have lunch with the Misters Loevy at their home.…The brothers were collectors of fine china and the walls of the dining room and two other rooms were literally covered with the loveliest rare old dishes and cups and saucers.… Brother Marcus took us in charge and showed us his collection of rare books, and never have I seen such a collection outside of the British Museum. He had two rooms whose walls were lined with bulging and loaded-down bookshelves. Books were stacked in all the corners of the rooms, and books overflowed the tables and chairs. For two hours we stood while we looked at them, for there was literally not an inch of space to sit on…everywhere were more books! And what books they were! There were the rarest and most ancient of books; there were the finest prints and engravings; there were autographed volumes and first editions; there were limited editions and de luxe editions; there were books whose only counterparts were in the British Museum, and a few which even the Museum doesn't own. Then there was a collection of autographed letters…letters from every King or Emperor of importance in history, letters from Popes and statesmen and authors. I think the only thing that man doesn't own is a First Edition of the Ten Commandments.

We only had time to glance hastily over the rest of their treasures…steel engravings, old sporting prints, Chinese embroidered brocades, cloisonne jars, tapestries and just about everything else there is. Then we listened to some splendid phonograph records, with a couple of jazz ones slipped in by Brother Sam who seems to lean more to the bright lights than to antiques (or would like you to think so) and then we had to tear ourselves away, for it was getting so late….

La Pulqueria, Mexico City. Alma Lavenson

Borda Garden Inn, Cuernavaca, March 23

We have now found the Best Yet…. We arrived here at noon today for a three days' visit and are perfectly enchanted, delighted and charmed…. Mexico City is interesting and all that, but the quiet little villages are what we like, and this place is just adorable.

Local trains in Mexico have a habit of just lying down and going to sleep at least three times during every trip, always selecting the hottest and least interesting spot, and always arriving everywhere late. However…when we had climbed to the summit of the range which separates us from Mexico, we could look down on the entire valley below us…rolling green hills extending for miles and miles and occasionally dotted with little settlements and villages….

Now we are in semi-tropical country, much greener and more luxuriant in growth than any that we met yet…. Here everything grows riotously. We took such a beautiful drive in the cool of the late afternoon (it is quite hot here during the day) about the surrounding country, along roads hemmed in by stone walls over which bougainvillea simply spilled in perfect splashes of color. Hibiscus and pomegranates grow wild; red coffee berries make brilliant spots among the tangle of underbrush. Banana trees, mango trees and any number of bushes and shrubs whose names we don't know lend shade and coolness to the dusty roads…, designed more for the natives' bare feet than for automobiles….

Cuernavaca, much too early in the morning, March 24

This is another of those towns which doesn't believe in letting its guests sleep. At five o'clock they wake the army up, as the army lives just down the street, and they wake it by means of so much tooting on so many bugles it's kind of hard on neighboring travelers…. Then, just as you begin to doze off after getting the army up, the churches begin….

For the afternoon we had planned a trip to the Floating Gardens of Xochimilco…. Originally the Floating Gardens really did float…they were made of reeds and twigs woven together and covered with earth. On these the Indians built little huts and planted vegetables and flowers, thus making a complete little estate that could be easily moved about. In the course of years the gardens have taken root, and are now merely a series of canals through the vegetable gardens that supply Mexico City with its calories. In the proper season, flowers are raised here too, and are said to present a riot of gorgeous coloring. At this time of the year,though, there were no flowers except calla lilies which looked far from riotous.

On the return trip [from the Floating Gardens] by streetcar, you pass, just before you reach Mexico, a flat plain from which "on a clear day" you may see Popocatepetl and Ixtaccihuatl.

Floating Gardens, Xochimilco. Alma Lavenson

We had driven out here several times by automobile, but each time had been able to see nothing but a hazy, indistinct outline in the distance. This evening, too, the mountains were hidden, until the sinking sun reached a point where it suddenly pierced through the haze, and before our astonished eyes, the two snow-capped cones shone out like brilliant silver against the dull background of haze. For a few moments this lasted. Then the silver gradually turned to rose, and finally the rose faded, and the two peaks sank back behind the gray curtain from which they had so suddenly emerged, leaving us quite speechless with the beauty of it....

Puebla, March 28

Some day when I have lots of time, I'll tell you all the wrong information and wild goose chases we have met with in our Pursuit of Rivera. We have now discovered a young lady in the Public Library who's a friend of his and who told us he hasn't been out of town at all, and gave us a letter to him which we are to present next Wednesday. Can it be that success is finally in sight?...

Mancera Hotel, Mexico, April 1

At last we have actually met Rivera. We called upon him early this morning at his home, armed with the letter from the young lady at the Library.... We weren't at all sure how an Artistic Temperament feels toward Tourists so soon after breakfast. In spite of the early hour, he had already gone out when we arrived, but his very beautiful wife (if that's what she is) received us in a purple brocade dressing gown and slippers, and showed us his pictures, promising that he would return very soon. He had only about five oil paintings, as most of his time is being devoted to murals, and though our baskets seem to be most elastic in their capacity, I don't believe that I could get a mural in. There was one oil painting that I liked a great deal, but I was uncertain about the price, so I thought I'd better consult the authorities at home first. There were several others that were very interesting but for one reason or another didn't seem just appropriate for…father to donate to Mills!

At any rate, I got two sketches for him to give instead…one large crayon one which is perfectly beautiful, and a smaller pen and ink, showing a typical…village scene. They may not be just what Mr. [Albert] Bender [a San Francisco collector] wanted but I felt safer about them, and he can always order the other painting if he wants. We were so enthusiastic about the sketches that we each got a small one for ourselves. Mine is a pencil sketch of the head of a *peón*…a perfectly lovely thing that I adore.

In the meantime, Rivera arrived home, and proved to be a great big, untidy creature, about 38 years old, with a very genial manner, a most interesting face, a perfectly child-like, pleasant smile, the worst fitting suit in the world, and little spikes of hair sticking up all over his head. He had nothing of the temperamental genius about him, and was much more pleasant than was necessary to us.

He asked us if we had seen his murals, and when we told him we'd seen the ones in the Preparatory School, we discovered that we'd missed his best ones…the ones which are making him famous and which are in the building of the Secretary of Education. He offered to take us over there himself, which of course we accepted.… I wish we had found these before the ones we saw the other day, for they give one such a totally different impression! They are wonderfully interesting…beautiful in coloring and in his manner of grouping them in the available space and adapting them to the lines of the building. Our estimation of him went soaring way up when we saw these! The frescoes depict the lives of the *peones*…the various industries which they engage in, their religious rites and festivals. They are most unpopular here because of their exhalting the lower classes, and this accounts for the general lack of interest in them and our difficulty in getting any information about Rivera. Already, although the paintings aren't all finished yet, they are being scratched and defaced by the public! All this hostility doesn't seem to bother Rivera at all.… He doesn't seem to be a mercenary sort of an individual… he simply calmly goes ahead and paints what he feels and lets the public like it or dislike it as they please.…

It being the eve of Holy Thursday, the streets were crowded and animated as we walked home in the dark [from the National Theater]…merry-go-rounds and carousels were being set up for the holidays and the whole town had a festive look. In doorways, almost beneath the feet of the many passersby, slept beggars who have come into the city in large numbers to haunt the church doors during Holy Week…women clad in masses of rags, with little children huddled close to them, sound asleep in all that noise and confusion.…

It is a most wonderful thing to watch the worshippers in the churches here, and no matter what your own religious beliefs may be, you can't help feeling most deeply moved by the devout and exhalted expressions of the kneeling Indians. The women, their heads covered by their dark blue rebozos, and the men with their big sombreros on the floor beside them, form a picture that you can't soon forget. They come just as they are, from whatever occupations they have…the vendors with their baskets of wares…the workmen in their ragged and patched overalls…the women with their children clinging to their skirts and tiny infants wrapped in their rebozos.…

This is Good Friday.… Tomorrow morning is another great event of Holy Week…the burning of Judas. All over town, effigies of him…most fantastic representations with ferocious grins, horns, and all sorts of wierd elaborations…stuffed with firecrackers, are hung up in the streets, and at ten o'clock they are set on fire. At the Alameda today, hundreds of the Judases were on sale in every shape and form and size from tiny ones to some six feet tall…all gayly colored…if not beautiful.…

Mexico City, Easter Sunday

This morning for the last time we were awakened by our neighborly rooster, aided by the cat and the dogs and the pigeons and the church bells. There was something awfully sad about realizing that never again would we be roused by those crows and barks and chimes. As we imbibed our last cup of spiced and foamy Mexican chocolate, it was all we could do to keep the tears from mingling with it. But we had not time to weep, for this was Easter Sunday, and we had a visit to pay to the Cathedral before our train left.…

(Right) Self-Portrait, 1932. Alma Lavenson

Biographical Chronology 1897–1989

Titles of photographs are listed as cited in the original exhibitions.

Albert Lavenson at The Lace House, c. 1890. Photographer unknown

Amy Furth Lavenson, 1894. Thors Studio, San Francisco

1897

• Alma Ruth Lavenson is born May 20 in San Francisco, the only child of Albert S. Lavenson and Amy Furth Lavenson.

• Albert Lavenson was born December 5, 1865, in Sacramento, one of eight children of Samuel and Caroline Lavenson, who emigrated in 1851 from Frankfurt, Germany. Samuel Lavenson became a prominent pioneer merchant. Albert Lavenson moved to the Bay Area in 1890 and began to work as a bookkeeper for Harris C. Capwell, owner of The Lace House (later H. C. Capwell & Company), a small dry goods business located at 12th and Washington streets, Oakland. In 1892, he became Capwell's partner and vice-president of the firm. In 1894, Albert Lavenson married Amy Furth (b. July 25, 1868), daughter of Simon and Polixene Furth, who emigrated from Bohemia in 1850. Gold Rush merchant Simon Furth sold mining supplies and operated banks with a partner in the small mining settlement of North San Juan in Nevada County, California.

1897–1906

• Alma Lavenson lives with her parents, her grandmother Polixene Furth, and her bachelor uncle Charles Furth in San Francisco at 910 Ellis Street, near Van Ness Avenue. She is tutored at home for first grade and begins at Eddy Street School with second grade. At about age eight she begins wearing eyeglasses, prescribed in an attempt to cure headaches that continue until she is about seventy-five years old.

About age three, c. 1900. Photographer unknown

Age six, 1903. Postal card sent to her father at The Lace House: "Dear Papa, Isn't this a fine Joke, Alma Ruth."

1906

• While the April 18 earthquake and fire destroy much of the city, Lavenson and her family hurriedly leave their home. After camping for about a week with other refugees in tents at the Presidio in San Francisco, they take a makeshift ferry to Oakland where they find temporary housing with about fourteen people in a house at 12th and Linden streets. Lavenson finds this all a big adventure and enjoys her first automobile ride, ferry ride, and camping experience.
• Albert Lavenson purchases a house at 657 Walsworth Avenue (now 3921 Harrison Street), Oakland.

1906-1915

• With no public school within walking distance, and because her mother does not want her to take streetcars, Lavenson attends The Horton School, a private grammar school on 12th Street in Oakland. After graduating she attends Oakland High School, at 12th and Jefferson streets, downtown Oakland.
• On Saturdays Lavenson accompanies her grandmother to San Francisco on the Key Route train, ferry, and streetcar. While her grandmother attends Saturday morning services at Temple Emanuel, Lavenson takes piano lessons with Oscar Weil, a noted classical musician/composer. Her weekly ritual with her grandmother includes lunch at the Golden Pheasant restaurant and a matinee at the Alcazar theater.
• Lavenson joins a piano class for eight hands in San Francisco, conducted by Emil Barth. She takes lessons until she enters college and continues to play with the eight-hands group until the birth of her first child.
• In 1912, the Capwell department store moves to a large building at 14th and Clay streets, downtown Oakland. It features a Venetian roof garden, tea room, children's play room, and promenade from which one can view the city. Albert Lavenson, an advertising and merchandising innovator, is largely responsible for the store's prosperity and enjoys a warm relationship with his employees. He becomes a major civic, cultural, religious, and philanthropic leader in Oakland.

1916-1919

• Alma Lavenson continues to live at home while attending the University of California, Berkeley, and is graduated in 1919 with a B.A. degree in psychology. Among her first photographs are snapshots of family and friends made with a folding Kodak.

1919-1922

• Lavenson learns to drive, and her father buys her a two-seater red Buick sports car.
• Lavenson volunteers at the pediatric clinic of the Public Health Center, Oakland. She administers intelligence tests to children with "low mentality" and interviews parents to arrange help for the children. When Lavenson is offered a part-time salaried position at the clinic, she accepts but returns the monthly paycheck because her father will not let her accept payment for work.
• During these years she meets Matt Wahrhaftig (b. April 5, 1892), a young attorney, whom she later marries. He is the youngest of four sons of Peter and Leah Wahrhaftig, who emigrated from Kovel, Russia, in 1890 and settled in Orangevale (Sacramento County), California, where they lived and worked in a farm colony.

With her first camera, c. 1918. Photographer unknown

With her father, c. 1915. Photographer unknown

1922

• Alma Lavenson embarks on a seven-month Grand Tour of Europe with her parents, her aunt Eugenie Dinkelspiel, and her cousin Amy. They visit France, Italy, Austria, Switzerland, Germany, Belgium, and England. Her earliest existing photographic negatives are tourist snapshots made with her Kodak camera during this trip. These include pictures of her family and points of interest: cathedrals, monuments, and scenic views.

1923

• Upon her return, and for a number of years, Lavenson works with her father on fundraising campaigns for the Oakland Community Chest. She continues to take piano lessons and to photograph.

• She learns to develop and print her own negatives by watching a technician at Bowman's drugstore, Oakland, go through the procedure. This is the full extent of her formal photographic training. With help from a friend, who gives her a homemade enlarger, she transforms a backyard childhood playhouse into a primitive darkroom. She avidly reads photography magazines and books on composition.

• Around this time, Lavenson purchases a 3¼ x 4¼ Ensign Popular Reflex camera, which comes with a sharp-focus lens. To achieve the soft-focus effects advocated by current pictorial publications, she abandons the sharp lens and purchases a second-hand Waterbury uncorrected lens.

1924

• Lavenson travels with her family by steamer from San Francisco to Hawaii. During the same year, she visits Glacier National Park, Montana. In both places, she makes poetic landscape photographs.

1926

• Lavenson photographs boats, dock workers, ships, and industrial subjects at the Oakland Estuary.

• When Lavenson makes plans to travel to Mexico with a girl friend, her family's close friend, San Francisco art patron Albert Bender, advises her to buy work by Mexican muralist/painter Diego Rivera. On Bender's recommendation, Lavenson's father instructs her to select a painting to donate to Mills College, Oakland.

After much perseverance, she locates Rivera and selects a painting, some drawings for Albert Bender, and one for herself. She photographs primarily architecture: churches, market places, and *pulquerías.*

• When Albert Lavenson announces his retirement, his employees refurnish his office, inducing him to maintain a place at the store. Their gift comes before any member of the store's staff learns that Lavenson has quietly arranged to divide $100,000 among seventy-two employees who, for ten years or more, have been his co-workers. Lavenson remains an influential leader in the commercial and cultural life of Alameda County.

1927

• Alma Lavenson makes landscape photographs in Zion National Park, Utah, and enters a photograph, her first submission, in the Beginners' Competition of *Photo-Era Magazine.* To her surprise, *The Light Beyond,* later titled *Zion Canyon,* is reproduced on the cover and as the frontispiece of the December issue. During the next five years, her photographs are frequently selected for publication in *Photo-Era Magazine* and in *Camera Craft.*

First published photograph, 1927. Alma Lavenson

In St. Mark's Square, Venice, 1922.
Photographer unknown

1928

• In April, Lavenson makes her first of many trips to the Southwest and photographs at Taos and Chaco Canyon, New Mexico, and at Mesa Verde, Colorado. Again her photographic subjects are primarily architectural: churches, adobe dwellings, kivas, and burial grounds.

1929

• Lavenson is in charge of "Special Features" for the Community Chest and makes photographs to illustrate campaign brochures and for use in advertisements.

1930

• Alma Lavenson makes her first photographs in the Mother Lode country, including images of her mother's childhood home in North San Juan. She also photographs in Yosemite National Park.

• Her work is included in national and international pictorialist salons in Los Angeles, Pittsburgh, Portland, Chicago, Rochester, London, Paris, and Torino.

• On March 12, Albert Lavenson is honored at the largest city-wide testimonial banquet ever sponsored in Oakland. He is honored as "one of the community's most beloved and most outstanding citizens." Numerous articles appear in local newspapers praising his many contributions to the city of Oakland.

• On June 8, Albert Lavenson suffers a heart attack and dies.

• When visiting the Lavenson household to offer his condolences, Albert Bender gives Alma Lavenson letters of introduction to three photographers: Edward Weston, Imogen Cunningham, and Consuelo Kanaga. Lavenson meets Kanaga, who becomes a friend, and Cunningham, who becomes a lifelong friend and the major photographic influence on her work. The three women often photograph together. Lavenson visits Weston in Carmel to seek his criticism of her photographs.

1931

• Lavenson exhibits in national and international pictorialist salons in Syracuse, Los Angeles, San Diego, Chicago, London, Dublin, Antwerp, and Paris.

1932

• Alma Lavenson's first one-person exhibition is held at the galleries of the California Camera Club in San Francisco in April.

• In June, four of her photographs are included in the international invitational exhibition *Showing of Hands,* organized by Lloyd Rollins, director of the M. H. de Young Memorial Museum, San Francisco. Among the other photographers represented are Berenice Abbott, Ansel Adams, Fred Archer, Margaret Bourke-White, Anton Bruehl, Clarence Sinclair Bull, Will Connell, Imogen Cunningham, Mary Jeanette Edwards, Walker Evans, Arnold Genthe, Consuelo Kanaga, Man Ray, Lee Miller, Laszlo Moholy-Nagy, Thurman Rotan, Edward Steichen, Roger Sturtevant, Maurice Tabard, Doris Ulmann, and Willard Van Dyke. Lavenson exhibits *Child with a Doll, Hands of Sydney Mitchell, Photographer at Work (Self-Portrait),* and *Hands of a Child,* all made in April in response to the call for entries.

• Lavenson receives second prize ($75) for her photograph *Snow Blossom* (1932) in an exhibition and competition, *California Trees Photographic Competition.* Of the 800 prints submitted, 160 are selected for exhibition at the de Young Museum. First prize ($100) goes to Edward Weston; Ansel Adams receives fourth, and Willard Van Dyke, seventh. Lavenson also exhibits *Danse Macabre.*

Albert Bender, c. 1930. Consuelo Kanaga

Snow Blossoms, 1932. Alma Lavenson

• In November, the inaugural museum exhibition of Group f/64 is held at the de Young Museum. This landmark exhibit champions straight photography, establishes a link to modernism, and creates an historical legacy of contributions by West Coast photographers. Included are the seven founding members—Ansel Adams, Imogen Cunningham, John Paul Edwards, Sonya Noskowiak, Henry Swift, Willard Van Dyke, and Edward Weston—and invited colleagues Preston Holder, Consuelo Kanaga, Alma Lavenson, and Brett Weston. Alma Lavenson exhibits four photographs: *Portrait of a Child* (1932), *Composition* (1931), *Gas Tank* (1931), and *Easter Lily* (1932).

1933

• The Brooklyn Institute of Arts and Sciences (now The Brooklyn Museum) gives Alma Lavenson her first one-person museum exhibition in February. She exhibits about fifty photographs: portraits, plants, still lifes, industrial and architectural studies, and landscapes.

• In April, she is given her first West Coast museum exhibition at the de Young Museum. She exhibits more than sixty photographs— plants and industrial studies.

• She marries Matt Wahrhaftig on September 6. They rent a house at 1109 Clarendon Crescent, Oakland. Although her legal name is now Wahrhaftig, she uses her maiden name, Lavenson, for all photography work. Matt Wahrhaftig is now a senior partner in the law firm of McKee, Tasheira and Wahrhaftig, in Oakland.

1934

• In April, Alma Lavenson is given a one-person exhibition at the 683 Brockhurst gallery, Oakland, the studio/gallery of Willard Van Dyke and former home of photographer and Photo-Secession member Anne Brigman. Lavenson exhibits twenty photographs, primarily industrial and plant studies.

• Lavenson joins the San Francisco Society of Women Artists. She participates in their annual juried exhibitions until 1970 and receives frequent awards for her work.

FROM TIME TO TIME VARIOUS OTHER PHOTOGRAPHERS WILL BE ASKED TO DISPLAY THEIR WORK WITH GROUP *f*.64

THOSE INVITED FOR THE FIRST SHOWING ARE:

PRESTON HOLDER
CONSUELA KANAGA
ALMA LAVENSON
BRETT WESTON

GROUP *f*.64

(ANSEL EASTON ADAMS
IMOGEN CUNNINGHAM
JOHN PAUL EDWARDS
SONYA NOSKOWIAK
HENRY SWIFT
WILLARD VAN DYKE
EDWARD WESTON)

ANNOUNCES AN EXHIBITION OF PHOTOGRAPHS AT THE M. H. DeYOUNG MEMORIAL MUSEUM FROM NOVEMBER FIFTEENTH THROUGH DECEMBER THIRTY-FIRST, NINETEEN THIRTY-TWO

Group f/64 exhibition. Announcement for 1932 exhibition.

Matt Wahrhaftig, 1933. Alma Lavenson

1935

• Lavenson makes photographs of Sydney Mitchell's Berkeley hills' gardens which are used to illustrate Mitchell's book *From A Sunset Garden: Essays for Any Adventurous Gardener.*
• Her first son, Albert, is born on October 2.
• Lavenson and her husband hire two architect friends to design a house in Piedmont, adjacent to Oakland. In November, Lavenson and her family move into their new home at 58 Wildwood Gardens, Piedmont. Matt Wahrhaftig, an experienced gardener, creates a garden and propagates orchids.

1937

• At Imogen Cunningham's insistence, Lavenson, while visiting New York City with her husband, shows a selection of her photographs to Alfred Stieglitz at An American Place, his gallery. Stieglitz grudgingly looks at the work, noting merely, "They're better than average."

1938

• Lavenson's son Paul is born on January 7.

1940

• For the Golden Gate International Exposition on Treasure Island in San Francisco in 1940, Ansel Adams organizes exhibitions for six galleries of photography, collectively titled *A Pageant of Photography.* He includes ten photographs of the Mother Lode and Virginia City by Alma Lavenson for the exhibition *California Women Photographers.* Also represented are: Sibyl Anakeef, Imogen Cunningham, Mary Jeanette Edwards, Sonia Noskowiak, and Marion Partridge.
• Lavenson continues to photograph extensively in the Mother Lode country and Virginia City. She writes an article, "Virginia City, Photographing a 'Ghost Town,'" illustrated with five of her photographs, for *U.S. Camera Magazine.*

1941

• With her husband, Alma Lavenson travels to New Mexico where she photographs pueblo dwellings, landscapes, Native Americans, and churches including Ranchos de Taos.
• She is awarded third prize for her photograph *San Ildefonso Indians* (1941) in the *First Annual Salon: Photography West of the Rockies* at the San Francisco Museum of Art. This photograph later becomes her most well known and frequently published.
• Lavenson is included in the traveling exhibition *Image of Freedom,* curated by Beaumont Newhall at the Museum of Modern Art, New York. She responds to a national solicitation and her photograph *Clouds, New Mexico* (1941) is among the ninety-five selected from more than 700 submitted for exhibition and purchase by the Museum's Department of Photography. Members of the jury include Ansel Adams, Alfred H. Barr, Jr., A. Hyatt Mayor, David H. McAlpin, Beaumont Newhall, Nancy Newhall, James Thrall Soby, and Monroe Wheeler.
• She attends a week-long informal photography workshop taught by Ansel Adams in Yosemite National Park in June. When Adams recommends that she use a 4 x 5 camera, Lavenson purchases a Crown View camera and begins to photograph with it while still in Yosemite.
• She also purchases a 2¼ x 2¼ Rolleiflex camera.

Sons Albert and Paul on Treasure Island, 1940. Alma Lavenson

Ansel Adams, Yosemite, 1941. Alma Lavenson

Church at Ranchos de Taos, New Mexico, 1941. Alma Lavenson

93

1942

• In her first of three one-person exhibitions at the San Francisco Museum of Art, *Photographs by Alma Lavenson,* Lavenson exhibits recent architectural studies of the Mother Lode and the Southwest.

1946

• In August, Ansel Adams and Minor White announce the beginning of an evening course for advanced photographers in the new Department of Photography, founded by Adams, at the California School of Fine Arts (now the San Francisco Art Institute) in San Francisco. The program, planned and taught by White, includes lectures, demonstrations, and criticism by Ansel Adams, Imogen Cunningham, and Alma Lavenson, who lectures on architectural photography.

• Lavenson begins to experiment with 4 x 5 color transparencies. She makes color images of nature and architecture in Monterey and the Mother Lode. Over the years she makes hundreds of color transparencies and slides of plants and flowers.

1947

• Alma Lavenson's color photographs of Sydney Mitchell's garden are published as a portfolio that illustrates his new book, *Your California Garden and Mine.*

• Lavenson continues to photograph the Mother Lode towns and makes inquiries to publishers about a proposed book. Her husband writes an essay on the Mother Lode to be used as the introduction.

1948

• Her second one-person exhibition, *Photographs by Alma Lavenson,* at the San Francisco Museum of Art, features recent photographs of the Mother Lode.

• Lavenson travels to the Caribbean with her husband.

1951

• Lavenson's mother, Amy Lavenson, who lives across the street from her daughter on Wildwood Gardens, dies on September 23.

1952

• Alma Lavenson enrolls as a sustaining subscriber to *Aperture* magazine, founded in 1952 in San Francisco and edited by Minor White. Some years later, she becomes disinterested in the magazine's content and decides not to renew her subscription. Imogen Cunningham tells her that the publication is important and renews Lavenson's subscription.

1955

• Alma Lavenson's photograph *San Ildefonso Indians* (1941) is included in *The Family of Man* exhibition curated by Edward Steichen, director of the Department of Photography, The Museum of Modern Art, New York, and the publication that accompanied it. Six editions of this exhibition travel internationally and are viewed by record-breaking crowds. Steichen so dictates the structure of this exhibition that the photographers, including Lavenson, lend their negatives for printing under his supervision.

• Matt Wahrhaftig, Lavenson's husband, is in poor health. Lavenson's interest in Braille begins at this time when she is looking for something to do while keeping her husband company at home. She transcribes books sent by the Library of Congress to the Berkeley Red Cross.

With her husband, c. 1950. Photographer unknown

West Coast prejury photograph selection with Edward Steichen for the *Family of Man* exhibition, at Wayne Miller's home in Orinda, California, March 28, 1954. *Left to right seated*: Steichen, Lavenson, Dorothea Lange; *standing*: Miller holding daughter Dana, Minor White, Milton Halberstadt, Imogen Cunningham, and two unidentified people. Photographer unknown

1957

• Lavenson and her husband travel to Hawaii.
• Matt Wahrhaftig, prominent in Bay Area legal circles and respected for his community leadership and legal wisdom, dies on May 13. Alma Lavenson is deeply saddened by her husband's death, and, while living alone for the remaining thirty-two years of her life, she often expresses regret that they did not marry sooner and have more years together.
• She attends the Bach Festival in Carmel, California, with friends for a week each summer until 1986.

1959

• Shortly after her husband's death, Lavenson becomes involved in a number of civic and cultural activities. She resumes transcribing books into Braille for high school students and for the Library of Congress, and she volunteers in a Braille book bindery. For ten years she also teaches weekly sessions of her eight-month Braille course at the Berkeley Red Cross to prepare prospective Braillers for certification by the Library of Congress.
• As a founding member of the Oakland Symphony Guild, Alma Lavenson attends Guild meetings and Symphony concerts regularly. She also works in the Oakland Symphony's music library, organizing and copying music scores for the musicians before each concert. She is especially interested in the annual Young Artists Award Competition, where young musicians from all over the world compete for prize money and an opportunity to perform with the orchestra. For many years, she hosts a visiting contestant for about ten days of rehearsals and auditions. She works on this annual event through 1972, when it is discontinued.
• While traveling in Guatemala and Mexico, Lavenson visits her son Albert who is conducting anthropological field research in Chiapas, Mexico. Her son Paul joins them.

1960

• *Photographs of a Vanishing Life* is Lavenson's third one-person exhibition at the San Francisco Museum of Art.

1962

• Lavenson travels and photographs in the Caribbean and in England, Scotland, Denmark, Spain, Sweden, Madeira, Majorca, Portugal, Norway, and Tangiers.

1963

• The *Photography in the Fine Arts IV* collection and exhibition, directed by Ivan Dmitri, opens at The Metropolitan Museum, New York, and travels nationally. Two of Lavenson's photographs, *Spiral, Tomar, Portugal* (1962) and *Noontime Rest* (1962), are among the 152 images selected from 1042 prints submitted. The Selection Committee, headed by Beaumont Newhall, includes photographers Ansel Adams and Ralph Steiner.
• Lavenson's work is included in the exhibition *The Henry Swift Memorial Collection,* at the San Francisco Museum of Art. George M. Craven, photography instructor at Foothill College, Los Altos, California, writes a paper, "The Group f/64 Controversy," as an introduction to the collection and exhibition. When Henry Swift died in 1962, his wife, Florence Alston Swift, with photographers Imogen Cunningham and Donald Ross, added more recent images by members of Group f/64 to broaden her husband's collection of photographs and donated the works to the San Francisco Museum of Art.

1965

• Lavenson travels and photographs in Asia: Bangkok, Calcutta, Cambodia, Ceylon, India, Japan, Kashmir, Malaya, Nepal, Taiwan, New Zealand, Philippines, and Singapore.

1967

• Lavenson travels and photographs in Greece, Italy, and Turkey.

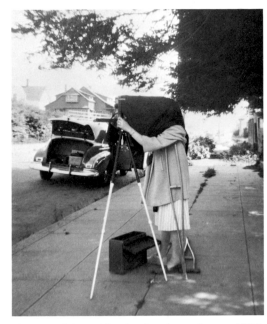

Photographing with tripod and crutches, c. 1950. Photographer unknown

Riding a camel in Tangiers, 1962. Photographer unknown

1969–1970

• Alma Lavenson travels and photographs in Africa.

• A selection of Lavenson's African photographs is included in the exhibition *Three Photographers and the Place* at Focus Gallery in San Francisco, with photographs by Charles Sanders and George Tice. This exhibition is Lavenson's first in a commercial gallery.

• Alma Lavenson supports The Oakland Museum as an active member of The Women's Board of The Oakland Museum Association from 1969 to 1987. She makes significant donations of her photography, and gives donations in honor of other women photographers, over some twenty-five years. She also volunteers in the Museum's Collector's Gallery. Lavenson's involvement as a patron and dedicated volunteer continues until 1988.

• For the Oakland Symphony's Young Artist Award Competition, Lavenson serves on the competition committee, assists with the auditions, photographs the competition, and hosts a musician.

• About twelve of Lavenson's former Braille students propose a monthly gathering to support their independent transcription. Lavenson attends the meetings for twenty years; she goes to one only a few days before she dies.

1971

• Lavenson travels and photographs in South America.

1976

• Alma Lavenson is deeply saddened by the death of her close friend Imogen Cunningham on June 24. Minor White also dies on that day.

• She travels and photographs in Central America, Guatemala, and Mexico.

1977

• Alma Lavenson's children give her a party to celebrate her eightieth birthday.

• Lavenson serves on the Advisory Committee of the Western Jewish History Committee of the Judah L. Magnes Museum, Berkeley, until 1986.

• She travels and photographs in Israel.

1978

• Five photographs by Alma Lavenson are included in the traveling exhibition *Group f/64*, organized by Jean S. Tucker for the University of Missouri-St. Louis. These include *Portrait of Imogen Cunningham* (1945) and the four images she exhibited in the Group's 1932 exhibition at the de Young Museum. The historic exhibition of photographs by the members and associates of Group f/64 causes renewed interest in this classic photographic tradition and in Alma Lavenson's photographs.

Grandchildren Solomon, Leah, Matt, Rebekah, and Esther, 1977. Alma Lavenson

Pondo Girl, South Africa, 1969. Alma Lavenson

1979

• Alma Lavenson receives the Dorothea Lange Award to an Outstanding Woman Photographer given by The Oakland Museum.

• Her first retrospective exhibition and publication, *Alma Lavenson,* is organized by The California Museum of Photography, Riverside, California. Joe Deal, curator of the museum, and guest curator Patricia G. Fuller make two visits to Lavenson's home to select photographs and interview her. The traveling exhibition and the publication are supported by a grant from the National Endowment for the Arts.

1979-1981

• Alma Lavenson and historian Richard Dillon plan a book of Lavenson's Mother Lode photographs. They sign a book contract with Northland Press, Flagstaff, Arizona, for a book to be published in April 1981. When the book's editor leaves the press in February 1981, Lavenson receives a letter notifying her that the book has been canceled. The book is never published.

1982

• Four industrial photographs by Alma Lavenson are included in the traveling exhibition and catalog *Images of America: Precisionist Paintings and Modern Photography,* organized by the San Francisco Museum of Modern Art. She exhibits *Gas Tanks* (1931/1979), *Union Oil Co. Tanks* (1931), *Calaveras Cement Works* (1933), and *Carquinez Bridge* (1933). This exhibit and publication provide a significant context for her urban and industrial photographs, seen in relation to the modernist precisionist movement.

1983

• Lavenson asks Susan Ehrens to help organize all her photographic work; together they archive, catalog, and document all photographic prints and negatives. Lavenson decides to sell her vintage prints to museums and private collectors.

• She travels with friends Joan Dunbar, Maurine Dunn, and Mary Hornberger to Maui.

1984

• Lavenson's photograph *San Ildefonso Indians* (1941) is included in an exhibition and publication, *Facets of the Collection: Faces Photographed,* to celebrate the fiftieth anniversary of the San Francisco Museum of Modern Art. She travels and photographs in Mexico.

1985

• Lavenson receives the Award of Honor for Outstanding Achievement in Photography from the San Francisco Arts Commission. She attends the award dinner with her son Albert. Other honorees include Bruce Conner, film; Manuel Neri, sculpture; and Alice Walker, literature.

1986

• Alma Lavenson participates in a symposium, "Founders of Modern Bay Area Photography," at The Oakland Museum with Ruth Bernhard, John Gutmann, Pirkle Jones, and guest speaker Charis Wilson Weston on March 9.

• The Department of Photographs of The J. Paul Getty Museum, Malibu, California, founded in mid-1984 with the acquisition of several major private collections, purchases five of Lavenson's photographs.

• Lavenson begins to devote more time to her photographic activities and decreases her volunteer work. She continues to attend the Oakland Symphony, the San Francisco Symphony matinee concerts, and monthly meetings of the "Braille Group."

Receiving silver brooch, symbol of The Oakland Museum's Dorothea Lange award from Helen Johnston of the Focus Gallery, at the opening of Lavenson's retrospective, The Oakland Museum, 1979. Photographer unknown

Age eighty-three, 1980. Joan Dunbar

Carousel Horses, 1981. Alma Lavenson

1987

- Learning that her fifty-year-old enlarger cannot be repaired, Lavenson purchases a new one.
- In April, after recent cataract surgery, Lavenson returns to New Mexico for the last time with friends Joan Dunbar, Maurine Dunn, and Mary Hornberger.
- Virginia Adams invites Alma Lavenson to dinner at her home in Carmel on May 1, before Lavenson attends an opening reception celebrating her exhibition, *Alma Lavenson, A Ninetieth Birthday Retrospective,* at The Friends of Photography, Carmel.
- Later that month, she celebrates her ninetieth birthday with a party at her home attended by family and close friends. With her sons, their wives, and her five grandchildren, she visits her exhibition in Carmel.
- For the first time since 1957, Lavenson's health does not permit her annual week-long visit to the Carmel Bach Festival. Her son Albert takes her to the festival for two days.

1988

- *Alma Lavenson Photographs,* her first one-person exhibition on the East Coast since 1933, features her vintage photographs of the 1920s and 1930s. Susan Ehrens is invited to curate the exhibition by Jay Fisher for The Baltimore Museum of Art, which acquires a selection of Lavenson's photographs.
- Lavenson's work is included in numerous exhibitions of women photographers of the 1920s and 1930s in Chicago, New York, San Francisco, and Zurich.
- After Lavenson suffers a mild stroke and as other signs of illness appear, family members arrange for home care and visit frequently.

1989

- On January 29, The Oakland Museum Art Department sponsors in Lavenson's honor a lecture, "f/64 and the California Contribution to Photography," by photohistorian Naomi Rosenblum.
- Lavenson's photographs are included in museum and gallery exhibitions in celebration of the 150th anniversary of photography.
- Lavenson's photograph *Tank* (1931) is included in *Legacy: Northern California's Photographic Tradition,* among the inaugural exhibitions of The Ansel Adams Center, San Francisco, new home of The Friends of Photography.
- Alma Lavenson suffers a second stroke and becomes seriously ill. She continues to meet with her "Braille Group" monthly and frequently goes to lunch with close friends. Despite her illness, she actively participates in the selection of photographs for her forthcoming book and enjoys visits from her family.
- On September 19, at age ninety-two, Alma Lavenson dies at her home.

Age eighty eight, 1985. Abe Aronow

Eucalyptus Tree, 1986. Alma Lavenson

(Right) Hands of the Iris Breeder (Sydney Mitchell), 1932. Alma Lavenson

Selected Exhibition History 1929–1990

Alma Lavenson's exhibition history, previously unpublished, serves as a record of her extensive participation in national and international exhibitions. This documentation was made possible because Lavenson kept detailed notebooks, scrapbooks, and clippings to record her activity as a photographer. Her records are an essential and primary source for this document, which includes a number of exhibitions for which no museum records exist. Where available, periodicals, exhibition catalogs, and brochures from public and private collections were used in checking accuracy and completing entries.

1929

Group Exhibition

First Rochester International Salon of Photography, The Memorial Art Gallery, December 5–January 5, 1930, one photograph. Catalog.

1930

Group Exhibitions

The Thirteenth International Salon of Photography, The Camera Pictorialists of Los Angeles, Los Angeles Museum, January, two photographs. Catalog.

Seventeenth Annual Pittsburgh Salon of Photographic Art, Carnegie Institute, March 22–April 29, one photograph. Catalog.

Thirty-first Annual Salon, Portland Society of Art, Portland, Maine, April, two photographs. Catalog.

Second International Salon of Chicago, Chicago Camera Club, May 1–June 1, one photograph. Catalog.

Second Pacific International Salon of Photographic Art, Museum of Art of Portland, Oregon, September 1–25, five photographs. Catalog,

London Salon of Photography: Seventy-fifth Annual Exhibition, Royal Photographic Society of Great Britain, London, England, September 13–October 11, three photographs. Catalog.

Second Pacific International Salon of Photographic Art, Art Galleries of the University of Oregon, Eugene, October 1–20.

XXV Salon International D'art Photographique, Société Française de Photographie, Paris, October, one photograph. Catalog.

Todmorden Photographic Society, November, four photographs. Catalog.

Second Rochester International Salon of Photography, The Memorial Art Gallery, December 4–January 4, 1931, two photographs. Catalog.

Terzo Salon Italiano d'Arte Fotografica Internazionale, Torino, Italy, December 20–January 11, 1931, two photographs. Catalog.

1931

Group Exhibitions

The Fourteenth International Salon of Photography, The Camera Pictorialists of Los Angeles, Los Angeles Museum, January 1–31, two photographs. Catalog.

Third Syracuse Salon, Syracuse Camera Club, January 2–31, three photographs. Catalog.

International Exhibition of Milan, Milan, Italy, April, one photograph. Catalog.

Thirty-second International Salon, Photo Section Annual Exhibition, Portland Society of Art, Portland, Maine, April 17–May 18, one photograph. Catalog.

First International Salon, Camera Enthusiasts of San Diego, May 1–20, two photographs. Catalog.

Wolverhampton Photographic Society, May, one photograph.

The All-American Photographic Salon, Los Angeles Museum, June 13–June 30, one photograph. Catalog.

The Third Chicago International Photographic Salon, under the auspices of the Chicago Camera Club, The Art Institute of Chicago, July 23–October 11, two photographs. Catalog.

Seventy-sixth Annual Exhibition, Royal Photographic Society of Great Britain, London, England, September 12–October 10, one photograph. Catalog.

XXVI Salon International D'art Photographique de Paris, La Société Française de Photographie and the Photo-club de Paris, Hôtel de La Société Française de Photographie, October 3–18, three photographs. Catalog.

Irish Salon, Third Annual Exhibition, Irish Salon of Photography, Mansion House, Dublin, Ireland, October, five photographs. Catalog.

Antwerp International Salon, Antwerp, Belgium, December, two photographs. Catalog.

1932

One-person Exhibition

California Camera Club, San Francisco, California, April 1–30.

Group Exhibitions

The Fifteenth Annual International Salon of Pictorial Photography, The Camera Pictorialists of Los Angeles, Museum of Science and Art, January 1–31, four photographs. Catalog.

Nineteenth Annual Pittsburgh Salon of Photographic Art, under the auspices of the Photographic Section of the Academy of Science and Art, Art Galleries of the Carnegie Institute, March 19–April 17, one photograph. Catalog.

First Annual Philadelphia International Salon of Photography, Philadelphia Museum of Art, March 26–April 11, two photographs. Catalog.

Second Annual International Salon of Photography, Fifth Annual Exhibition, Camera Enthusiasts of San Diego, Fine Arts Gallery, April 15–May 15, one photograph. Catalog.

Portland Society of Art, Portland, Maine, April, one photograph. Catalog.

Foto-en Studiekring, Antwerp, Belgium, four photographs. Catalog.

Showing of Hands, M. H. de Young Memorial Museum, San Francisco, June–July.

Chicago Camera Club, July, two photographs. Catalog.

Toronto Salon, Toronto, Canada, one photograph. Catalog.

Second Travel Salon of Pictorial Photographers, M. H. de Young Memorial Museum, San Francisco, August 20–September 20, two photographs.

California Trees Photographic Competition, M. H. de Young Memorial Museum, San Francisco, organized by The California Conservation Committee of the Garden Club of America with awards from the Save-the-Redwoods League, September 21–October 21, two photographs; second prize for *Snow Blossoms.*

Paris Salon, October, two photographs. Catalog.

Leipzig Salon, October, three photographs. Catalog.

Group f/64 Show, M. H. de Young Memorial Museum, San Francisco, November 15–January 1, 1933, four photographs.

1933

One-person Exhibitions

The Brooklyn Institute of Arts and Sciences (now The Brooklyn Museum), February.

Photographs by Alma R. Lavenson, M. H. de Young Memorial Museum, San Francisco, April 7–May 7.

Group Exhibitions

The Second International Salon of Photography, Philadelphia Museum of Art, May 6–June 26. Catalog.

Group f/64, *Ansel Adams Gallery,* San Francisco, September.

1934

One-person Exhibition

Photographs by Alma Lavenson, 683 Brockhurst gallery, Oakland, April 21–May 15.

Group Exhibition

San Francisco Society of Women Artists, M. H. de Young Memorial Museum, San Francisco, April 7–May 6.

1935

Group Exhibition

San Francisco Society of Women Artists, San Francisco Museum of Art (now the San Francisco Museum of Modern Art), November 15–December 14, four photographs. Catalog.

1936

Group Exhibitions

Bay Region Art Association Exhibition, March 14.

Twelfth Annual Exhibition, San Francisco Society of Women Artists, San Francisco Museum of Art, October 9-November 7, three photographs. Catalog.

Mills College Art Gallery, Oakland, October 25-December 2.

1937

Group Exhibition

Fourth International Salon by the Pictorial Photographers of America, American Museum of Natural History, New York, March 29-April 17, four photographs.

1938

Group Exhibition

Thirteenth Annual Exhibition, San Francisco Society of Women Artists, San Francisco Museum of Art, November 5-December 4, six photographs. Catalog.

1939

Group Exhibitions

Sixth International Salon of Photography, Centennial Exhibition, Pictorial Photographers of America, The World's Fair, American Museum of Natural History, New York, May 1-October 31, two photographs. Catalog.

Fourteenth Annual Exhibition, San Francisco Society of Women Artists, San Francisco Museum of Art, November 3-December 3, six photographs. Catalog.

1940

Group Exhibitions

A Pageant of Photography: California Women Photographers, Palace of Fine Arts, San Francisco Golden Gate International Exposition, Treasure Island, May 25-September 29. Book published on the occasion of the exhibition.

Fifteenth Annual Exhibition, San Francisco Society of Women Artists, San Francisco Museum of Art, November 7-December 8, twelve photographs. Catalog.

1941

Group Exhibitions

East Bay Art Association, Oakland, February, twelve photographs.

Mills College Art Gallery, Mills College, Oakland, February, five photographs.

First Annual Salon: Photography West of the Rockies, San Francisco Museum of Art, October 28-November 16, four photographs; third award for *San Ildefonso Indians.* Catalog.

Sixteenth Annual Exhibition, San Francisco Society of Women Artists, San Francisco Museum of Art, November 6-December 7, seven photographs. Catalog.

Image of Freedom, The Museum of Modern Art, New York, November-January, traveling exhibition.

1942

One-person Exhibition

Photographs by Alma Lavenson, San Francisco Museum of Art, June 3-15.

Group Exhibition

Seventeenth Annual Exhibition, San Francisco Society of Women Artists, San Francisco Museum of Art, November 12-December 13, six photographs; honorable mention for *Mendocino Home.* Catalog.

1943

One-person Exhibition

Berkeley Women's City Club, Berkeley, February 1-28.

Group Exhibitions

Image of Freedom, San Francisco Museum of Art, February 2-22, organized by The Museum of Modern Art, New York.

Eighteenth Annual Exhibition, San Francisco Society of Women Artists, San Francisco Museum of Art, November 17-December 12, six photographs; honorable mention for entire group. Catalog.

1944

Group Exhibitions

Photographs of 1943, circulated overseas by the Office of War Information.

Mills College Art Gallery, Oakland, October-November, twelve photographs.

Nineteenth Annual Exhibition, San Francisco Society of Women Artists, San Francisco Museum of Art, November 16-December 3, two photographs. Catalog.

1945

Group Exhibitions

Exhibition in Cairo, Office of War Information.

Twentieth Annual Exhibition, San Francisco Society of Women Artists, San Francisco Museum of Art, November 28- December 16, four photographs. Catalog.

1946

Group Exhibitions

Outdoor Art Show, San Francisco Art Commission Exhibition, Civic Center, October.

Twenty-first Annual Exhibition, San Francisco Society of Women Artists, San Francisco Museum of Art, November 8-December 1, six photographs; honorable mention for *Imogen Cunningham.* Catalog.

1947

Group Exhibitions

Twenty-second Annual Exhibition, San Francisco Women Artists (formerly San Francisco Society of Women Artists), San Francisco Museum of Modern Art, November 17-December 15, four photographs; award for *Palm Leaves.* Catalog.

1948

One-person Exhibition

Photographs by Alma Lavenson, San Francisco Museum of Art, July 26-August 29.

Group Exhibition

Twenty-third Annual San Francisco Women Artists, San Francisco Museum of Art, November 12-December 19, six photographs. Catalog.

1949

Group Exhibitions

The Library of Congress, Washington, D. C. Exhibition for the centennial of the California Gold Rush.

Twenty-fourth Annual San Francisco Women Artists, San Francisco Museum of Art, November 19-December 18, five photographs; award for *False Hellebore* (1949). Catalog.

1950

Group Exhibitions

Twenty Bay Region Photographers, San Francisco Museum of Art, June 19-July 16.

Twenty-fifth Annual San Francisco Women Artists, San Francisco Museum of Art, November 17-December 10, four photographs; honorable mention for *Farm Near Morro Bay.* Catalog.

1951

Group Exhibitions

Bay Area Photographers, Mills College Art Gallery, Oakland, California, April.

Twenty-sixth Annual San Francisco Women Artists, San Francisco Museum of Art, November 9-December 2, six photographs; honorable mention for *Church, Hornitos.* Catalog.

1952

Group Exhibition

Twenty-seventh Annual San Francisco Women Artists, San Francisco Museum of Art, November 14-December 7, six photographs. Catalog.

1953

Group Exhibitions

Bay Area Photographers, San Francisco Museum of Art, September.

Twenty-eighth Annual San Francisco Society of Women Artists, San Francisco Museum of Art, November 10-December 11, seven photographs; award for *Portrait in a Stable* and *Stable Boy.* Catalog.

1954

Group Exhibitions

Perceptions, San Francisco Museum of Art, August 10-September 17, one photograph. Catalog.

Twenty-ninth Annual San Francisco Society of Women Artists, San Francisco Museum of Art, November 13-December 5, five photographs; honorable mention for *Rock and Fence.* Catalog.

1955

Group Exhibitions

The Family of Man, The Museum of Modern Art, New York, traveling exhibition, one photograph. Book published on the occasion of the exhibition.

San Francisco Weekend, San Francisco Art Festival, September, two photographs.

Thirtieth Annual San Francisco Women Artists, San Francisco Museum of Modern Art, November 10-December 11, twelve photographs; award for *Basket Market, Jamaica;* honorable mention for *Market, Montego Bay,* and *Diving Boy.* Catalog.

1956

Group Exhibitions

San Francisco Discovery, Bay Area Photographers, May.

Thirty-first Annual San Francisco Women Artists, San Francisco Museum of Art, November 3-November 25, seven photographs. Catalog.

USIA exhibition in Warsaw; travels to Europe and Asia.

1957

Group Exhibitions

The Family of Man, Palace of the Legion of Honor, San Francisco, California, organized by The Museum of Modern Art, New York, January 26-May 8.

Thirty-second Annual San Francisco Society of Women Artists, San Francisco Museum of Art, November 16-December 8, eight photographs; prizes for three photographs. Catalog.

1958

Group Exhibition

Thirty-third Annual San Francisco Women Artists, San Francisco Museum of Art, November 8-30, one photograph. Catalog.

1960

One-person Exhibition

Photographs of a Vanishing Life, San Francisco Museum of Art, November 2-December 4.

Group Exhibition

Thirty-fifth Annual San Francisco Women Artists, San Francisco Museum of Art, October 28- December 4, thirteen photographs. Catalog.

1962

Group Exhibitions

Photography in the Fine Art IV, The Metropolitan Museum of Art, New York, traveling exhibition.

Thirty-sixth Annual San Francisco Women Artists, San Francisco Museum of Art, December 2-30, five photographs. Catalog.

1963

Group Exhibitions

The Henry Swift Collection of Photographs by the Group f/64, San Francisco Museum of Art, August 1-September 23.

Thirty-seventh Annual San Francisco Women Artists, San Francisco Museum of Art, December 14-January 12, three photographs. Catalog.

1964

Group Exhibition

Thirty-eighth Annual San Francisco Women Artists, San Francisco Museum of Art, November 13-December 13, one photograph. Catalog.

1965

Group Exhibition

Photography in the Fine Arts IV, M. H. de Young Memorial Museum, San Francisco, January 8-31.

1966

Group Exhibitions

f/64 and Before, Kaiser Center Gallery, Oakland, organized by The Oakland Art Museum, October 29-November 19.

Fortieth Annual San Francisco Women Artists, San Francisco Museum of Art, December 17-January 15, two photographs. Catalog.

1967

Group Exhibitions

Photography for the Art in the Embassies Program, Focus Gallery, San Francisco, California, co-sponsored with The Oakland Museum, September 6-30, traveling exhibition.

1968

Group Exhibitions

San Francisco Women Artists, Focus Gallery, San Francisco, March 5-30.

f/64 and Before, The Oakland Museum, October 29-November 29.

1970

Group Exhibitions

Three Photographers and the Place, Focus Gallery, San Francisco, March 3-28. With Charles Sanders and George Tice.

The Portrait in Photography, San Francisco Museum of Art, August 4-September 20, three photographs.

1972

Group Exhibition

Group f/64, Fine Arts Center, University of New Mexico, Albuquerque, March 19-April 16.

1973

Group Exhibition

Images of Imogen, Focus Gallery, San Francisco, April 3-May 5.

1976

Group Exhibition

Selections from the Permanent Collection of Photography, San Francisco Museum of Art, June 3-August 1.

1977

Group Exhibition

California Scenes, The Oakland Museum, April 5-May 29.

1978

Group Exhibitions

Group f/64, organized by the University of Missouri-St. Louis and exhibited at Gallery 210, Lucas Hall, University of Missouri-St. Louis, April 3-30; Gallery of Fine Arts, University of Missouri-Kansas City, May 7-31; Fine Arts Gallery, University of Missouri-Columbia, June 12-July 7; The Oakland Museum, July 18-September 10, five photographs. Catalog.

Photographs from the Permanent Collection, San Francisco Museum of Modern Art, April 20-June 11, one photograph.

1979

One-person Exhibition

Alma Lavenson, organized by the California Museum of Photography, Riverside California, and traveled to the University Art Gallery, University of California, Riverside, January 15-February 23; the University Art Museum, University of New Mexico, Albuquerque, March 2-April 13, and The Oakland Museum, in two parts: *The Early Years: 1927-1933,* October 9-28, and *People and Places: 1938-1969,* November 6-25. Catalog.

1980

Group Exhibition

Bay Area Photographers: 1954-1979, Focus Gallery, San Francisco, February 5-March 1.

1981

One-person Exhibition

Recent Photographs by Alma Lavenson, Focus Gallery, San Francisco, May 26-June 27.

Group Exhibition

California's Trees: A Selection of Photographs from the Exhibit of 1932, Morrison Library, University of California-Berkeley, April 1-May 29. Brochure.

1982

One-person Exhibition

[Photographs of the Mother Lode], Calaveras County Museum and Archives, San Andreas, California, June 29-August.

Group Exhibition

Images of America: Precisionist Paintings and Modern Photography, organized by the San Francisco Museum of Modern Art and exhibited there, September 9-November 7, and traveled to The Saint Louis Art Museum, December 6-January 30, 1983; The Baltimore Museum of Art, February 28-April 25; Des Moines Art Center, May 23-July 17; The Cleveland Museum of Art, August 15-October 9; four photographs. Catalog.

1983

One-person Exhibition

Alma Lavenson: 50 Years of Photography, University Press Books Gallery, Berkeley, October 22-December 2.

Group Exhibition

Facets of the Collection: From The California Sharp School, San Francisco Museum of Modern Art, September 9-October 30.

1984

Group Exhibition

Facets of the Collection: Faces Photographed, San Francisco Museum of Modern Art, December 9-March 24, 1985, one photograph. Catalog.

1986

Group Exhibitions

Portraits, Portland Art Museum, Portland, Oregon, February 5-April 6.

More Than Land or Sky: The Northern California Landscape, Ruben Salazar Library, Sonoma State University, April 23-May 30, one photograph. Catalog.

In Spite of Everything, Yes, organized by the Hood Museum of Art, Dartmouth College, Hanover, New Hampshire, August 30-October 26, and traveled to Meridian House International, Washington, D. C., June 25-September 10, 1987, and Center Gallery, Bucknell University, Louisburg, Pennsylvania, December 5-January 22, 1988, one photograph. Catalog.

1987

One-person Exhibition

Alma Lavenson: A Ninetieth Birthday Retrospective, The Friends of Photography, Sunset Cultural Center, Carmel, California, May 1-June 14.

Group Exhibitions

Group f/64, Jones Troyer Gallery, Washington, D.C., May 22-June 26.

Photographs from the Collection of Gary and Barbara Hansen, The Saint Louis Art Museum, Saint Louis, Missouri, June 23-August 9, one photograph. Catalog.

1988

One-person Exhibition

Alma Lavenson Photographs, The Baltimore Museum of Art, Baltimore, Maryland, March 8-April 24.

Group Exhibitions

Women of the 20s and 30s, Edwynn Houk Gallery, Chicago, Illinois, March 11-April 30, four photographs. Catalog.

Children of Our Times, A Photographic Essay 1900-1988, Stephen Wirtz Gallery, San Francisco, November 22-December 30, two photographs.

Photographs: A Child's World, Michael Shapiro Gallery, San Francisco, November 22-December 31, two photographs.

150 Years of Photography, Portland Art Museum, Portland, Oregon, December 2-January 29, 1989.

1989

Group Exhibitions

Women of the 20s and 30s, Anthony Ralph Gallery, New York, January 24-March 4, two photographs.

Women of the 20s and 30s, Galerie Zur Stockeregg, Zürich, Switzerland, January 25-March 9, two photographs.

A History of Photography from California Collections, San Francisco Museum of Modern Art, February 9-April 30, one photograph. Brochure.

Selections from the Gallery: 1920s and 1930s, Robert Koch Gallery, San Francisco, September 7-October 14, two photographs.

Seven Bay Area Women Photographers, Michael Shapiro Gallery, San Francisco, September 9-October 21, six photographs.

Legacy: Northern California's Photographic Tradition, The Friends of Photography, The Ansel Adams Center, San Francisco, September 17-November 5, one photograph.

Experimental Photography, The Machine Age, The J. Paul Getty Museum, Malibu, California, September 26-December 10, two photographs. Brochure.

1990

One-person Exhibition

Alma Lavenson, The Friends of Photography, The Ansel Adams Center, San Francisco, November 21-February 17, 1991.

Group Exhibition

Persistent Themes: Notable Photography Acquisitions, 1985-1990, The J. Paul Getty Museum, Malibu, California, June 5-September 2, one photograph. Brochure.

Selected Bibliography

Alma Lavenson's scrapbooks and files include newspaper and magazine clippings of her exhibition reviews and published photographs. Although these frequently provide pertinent source information, many times they do not give full bibliographic details. Other resources were used to make each entry as complete as possible.

Exhibition catalogs are identified by the abbreviation Ex. cat. Exhibition reviews are identified by the abbreviation Ex. rev. Exhibitions of the San Francisco Society of Women Artists are identified by the abbreviation SFWA.

Titles of photographs reproduced are listed as cited in the original publications and are in italics.

Works by Alma Lavenson

Alma Lavenson. Riverside: California Museum of Photography, 1979. Ex. cat.

Alma R. Lavenson. "Virginia City, Photographing a 'Ghost Town,'" U.S. Camera Magazine, Travel Issue, no. 10 (June-July 1940), pp. 52-53, 65-66. Article and five photographs.

Articles and Books Illustrated by Alma Lavenson

Mitchell, Sydney B. "Every Western Garden Calls for Flowering Trees," *Sunset,* Vol. 74, no. 4 (April 1935), pp. 11, 66-68.

____. *From a Sunset Garden,* New York: Doubleday, Doran & Company, Inc., 1932.

____. "The Story of My Own Sunset Garden," *Sunset,* Vol. 74, no. 2 (February 1935), pp. 16-17.

____. "Sunset Gold," *Sunset,* Vol. 74, no. 4 (April 1935), p. 4.

____. "Why I Chose These Trees for My Sunset Garden," *Sunset,* Vol. 74, no. 3 (March 1935), pp.18-19, 65.

____. *Your California Garden and Mine,* New York: M. Barrows and Company, Inc., 1947.

Photographic Reproductions in Periodicals

American Photography, Ninth Annual Competition, 1929. Honorable Mention, *Winter Hillside.*

American Photography, Tenth Annual Competition, 1930. Honorable Mention.

The American Annual of Photography 1932, Vol. 45, Boston: American Photographic Publishing Co., 1930, p. 87. *Winter Reflections.*

Aperture 11:4 (1964), *Photograph of Imogen Cunningham,* 1958. Issue devoted to the photography of Imogen Cunningham.

The Camera, Philadelphia, Vol. 37, no. 4 (October 1928), p. 239. *Marjorie.*

____. Vol. 41, no. 1 (July 1930), p. 17. *The Iron Balcony* from the 1930 *Pittsburgh Salon of Photographic Art.*

____. Vol. 41, no. 3 (September 1930), p. 144. *Winter Reflections* from the Thirty-first Annual Salon of the Portland Society of Art, Photographic Section, Portland, Maine.

____. Vol. 41, no. 6 (December 1930). *The Iron Balcony* from the 1930 Pacific International Salon of Photographic Art, Portland and Eugene, Oregon.

Camera Craft, San Francisco, Vol. 35, no. 7 (July 1928), p. 331. Third Prize, Advanced Competition, *Untitled* [snow scene].

____. Vol. 35, no. 8 (August 1928), p. 381. Fifth Award, Advanced Pictorial, *Untitled.*

____. Vol. 36, no. 1 (January 1929). *Winter.*

____. Vol. 36, no. 3 (March 1929), p. 131. Fifth Prize, Advanced Competition, *Untitled* [*Cliff Dwellings,* Mesa Verde, Colorado].

____. Vol. 36, no. 5 (May 1929), pp. 230, 235. Medal Award, Advanced Class, *Winter* [snow scene].

____. Vol. 36, no. 9 (September 1929), p. 433. Fifth Prize, Advanced Competition, *Untitled* [book end with lamp].

____. Vol. 36, no. 10 (October 1929), p. 482. Silver Medal Print, *Untitled* [*Porch Shadows,* Santa Barbara].

____. Vol. 37, no. 4 (April 1930), p. 185. Fourth Prize, Advanced Competition, *Untitled* [*Winter Reflections*].

____. Vol. 37, no. 6 (June 1930), p. 289. Fourth Prize, Advanced Competition, *Untitled* [snow scene].

____. Vol. 38, no. 4 (April 1931), p. 187. Second Prize, Advanced Competition, *Untitled* [*Composition in Glass*].

____. Vol. 44, no. 8 (August 1937), p. 375. *Wagon Wheel* from the 4th International Salon, Pictorial Photographers of America.

____. Vol. 48, no. 12 (December 1941), pp. 721-722. *San Ildefonso Indians* from the 1st Annual West of the Rockies Salon, San Francisco Museum of Art.

Modern Photography, London and New York: The Studio Ltd., 1931, p. 66. *Gas Tank.*

____. 1932, p. 97. *Untitled* [*Cows*].

The New York Times Magazine (June 29, 1930), p. 14. *Stone Walls Apparently Do Not a Schoolhouse Make* [Camp Wasibo for the Camp Fire Girls].

Photo-Era Magazine, New Hampshire. Vol. 59, no. 6 (December 1927), cover, frontispiece, p. 337. Honorable Mention, Beginners' Competition, *The Light Beyond,* Zion Canyon, 1927.

____. Vol. 61, no. 1 (July 1928), p. 101. Second Prize, Beginners' Competition, *The Winnower.*

____. Vol. 62, no. 5 (May 1929), pp. 269, 271-272. Second Prize, Beginners' Competition, Miscellaneous, *Mount Tamalpais.*

____. Vol. 62, no. 6 (June 1929), pp. 325, 328. Second Prize, Beginners' Competition, *Muchacho* [made in Zapopan, Mexico, in March].

____. Vol. 63, no. 2 (August 1929), pp. 97, 100. Second Prize, Beginners' Competition, Miscellaneous, *A Springtime Silhouette* [*Oak Trees*].

____. Vol. 63, no. 5 (November 1929), pp. 266, 271. Advanced Competition, Third Prize, Miscellaneous, *The Iron Balcony.*

____. Vol. 64, no. 3 (March 1930), pp. 146, 157. Honorable Mention, Miscellaneous Category, *Four and Twenty Blackbirds.*

____. Vol. 66, no. 5 (May 1931), p. 266. Honorable Mention, *Composition in Glass.*

U.S. Camera 1943, New York: Duell, Sloan & Pearce, 1943, p. 101. *San Ildefonso Indians.*

Exhibition Catalogs and Books

Craven, George M. "Group f/64 and Its Relations to Straight Photography in America." Unpublished master's thesis, Ohio University, 1958.

____. *The Group f/64 Controversy: An Introduction to the Henry F. Swift Memorial Collection of the San Francisco Museum of Modern Art,* San Francisco: San Francisco Museum of Art, 1963. Brochure.

Ehrens, Susan. *The Consolidated Freightways, Inc. Collection,* Palo Alto, California: Consolidated Freightways, Inc., 1988. *Tank Shadow* (1981), *Masts and Funnels* (1930), *Tank* (1933), *Stacks, Chevrolet Plant* (1933), *Two Tanks* (1983), *Tanks and Shadows, Alameda* (1984).

Facets of the Collection: Pacific Telesis Group. San Francisco: Pacific Telesis Group, 1988. *Carquinez Bridge,* p. 111.

The Family of Man. New York: The Museum of Modern Art, 1955. Ex. cat., *San Ildefonso Indians,* p. 206.

Group f/64. Albuquerque: University of New Mexico Art Museum, 1972. Ex. cat.

Group f/64. Saint Louis: University of Missouri, 1978. Ex. cat., pp. 32-35. *Gas Tank* (1931), *Portrait of a Child* (1931), *Easter Lily* (1932).

Images of America: Precisionist Painting and Modern Photography. San Francisco: San Francisco Museum of Modern Art, 1982. Ex. cat., pp. 99, 100, 104-5, 192-93, 224, 234. *Tanks—Union Oil Co.* (1931), plate 68; *Calaveras Cement Works* (1933), plate 69.

In Spite of Everything, Yes. Hanover, New Hampshire: Hood Museum of Art, Dartmouth College, 1986. Ex. cat., p. 148. *San Ildefonso Indians,* p. 43.

Journal, The J. Paul Getty Museum, Vol. 14 (1986), p. 284. Features acquisitions for 1985; *Self-Portrait* (1932).

A Pageant of Photography. San Francisco: S.F. Bay Exposition Co., 1940. Ex. cat., "*Food Products,*" Virginia City.

Perceptions. San Francisco: San Francisco Museum of Art, 1954. Ex. cat.

Photographs from the Collection of Gary and Barbara Hansen. Saint Louis: The Saint Louis Art Museum, 1987. Ex. cat., *Imogen Cunningham* (1945), p. 35.

The Pictorialist. Los Angeles: Camera Pictorialists, 1932, *Calla Leaves,* plate 25.

Picturing California: A Century of Photographic Genius. Oakland: The Oakland Museum, 1989. Ex. cat., *Church, Vallecito* (1983), p. 62.

Portrait of Artists, Faces Photographed. San Francisco: San Francisco Museum of Modern Art, 1985, p. 37. Ex. cat., *San Ildefonso Indians,* plate 19.

Sullivan, Constance, ed. *Women Photographers.* New York: Harry N. Abrams, Inc., Publishers, 1990. *Child with Doll* (1932), plate 53; *Egg Box* (1931), plate 54; *Calaveras Dam II* (1932), plate 55.

XXVIe Salon International d'Art Photographie de Paris. Société Française de Photographie, Paris: Braun & Cie, 1931, p. 41. Ex. cat., *Persimmons.*

Vintage Photographs by Women of the 20s and 30s. Chicago: Edwynn Houk Gallery, 1988, pp. 27, 42. Ex. cat., *Calaveras Dam* (1932), p. 27, *Water Lilies* (1932), p. 42.

Weston, Edward. *The Daybooks of Edward Weston,* Volume II: California 1927–1934 (edited by Nancy Newhall). New York: Horizon Press and Rochester, New York: George Eastman House, 1966, p. 265.

Critical Articles about Alma Lavenson

Adams, Ansel. "The Pageant of Photography," *Camera Craft,* Vol. 67, no. 9 (September 1940), pp. 437-446.

"Art Center Show at Palace," *San Francisco Examiner* (April 2, 1933), p. 6-E. Ex. rev.

Berg, Paul. "UMSL Brings Back Part of 1932 Show," *St. Louis Post-Dispatch* (April 2, 1978), Sunday Pictures Section, pp. 26-31. Ex. rev.

Berggruen, Heinz. "Vienna and Points West Represented in Art Shows," *San Francisco Chronicle* (November 13, 1938), *This World,* p. 28. Ex. rev.

Blum, Walter. "Testaments of an Era," *San Francisco Examiner & Chronicle,* September 3, 1978, California Living Magazine, pp. 7-9. Ex. rev.

Bolz, Carolyn. "Alma Lavenson—Pioneer of Modern Photography," *The Highlander* (January 25, 1978), p. 15. Feature article.

Bowles, Demetra. "Simple Forms and Layered Images," *Artweek,* Vol. 12, no. 22 (June 20, 1981), p. 11. Ex. rev., *Doll in a Window.*

"California Trees Competition," *Camera Craft* (November 1932), p. 481. Second prize.

"California's Trees," *American Forests* (January 1933), pp. 12-19. Ex. rev., *Snow Blossoms,* pp. 14. Second prize.

Corti, Walter Robert. "The Family of Man—*Wir Menschen,*" *Du,* Switzerland, no. 11 (November 1955), pp. 13-56. Issue devoted to *The Family of Man* exhibition; *San Ildefonso Indians,* p. 44.

"Dedicated Amateur," *The Museum of California,* The Oakland Museum (October 1979), pp. 8-9. Feature article; *Composition* (1931).

Dorsey, John. "Double Exposure at the BMA," *The Sun* (March 10, 1988), pp. 1F, 2F. Ex. rev.

Duffy, Robert W. "Major Photography Shows at Museum, UMSL," *St. Louis Post-Dispatch* (April 9, 1978), p. 5C. Ex. rev.

Dungan, H. L. "Exhibition by Women Artists Is Big Success," *Oakland Tribune* (November 26, 1933), pp. S-8. Ex. rev.

———. "Oakland Art Gallery's Annual Water Color Show Opens Today," *Oakland Tribune* (October 4, 1936), pp. B-6. Ex. rev.

———. "Photographers of California Hold Exhibit," *Oakland Tribune* (November 1, 1936), p. B-6. Ex. rev.

———. "Judges Enter Many Jury Free Works," *Oakland Tribune* (October 17, 1937), p. S-8. Ex. rev.

———. "Women Artists Are Radical Enough; Good Show in S.F.," *Oakland Tribune* (November 16, 1941), p. S-7. Ex. rev. SFWA.

———. "Women's Art Is Vigorous and Radical," *Oakland Tribune* (November 22, 1942), p. B-8. Ex. rev. SFWA.

———. "Women Artists Hold 18th Annual Exhibition," *Oakland Tribune* (November 21, 1943), p. B-2. Ex. rev. SFWA; Lavenson wins award.

———. "Sculpture Wins First Prize, Watercolor Next," *Oakland Tribune* (November 28, 1943), p. B-2. Ex. rev. SFWA.

———. "Bay Artists and Photographers Reveal Fine Achievements at Exhibit Praised by Critic," *Oakland Tribune* (September 5, 1948), p. C-3. Ex. rev.

———. "Oakland Gallery's Annual Show Set," *Oakland Tribune* (July 9, 1950), p. C-3. Ex. rev.

Edwards, John Paul. "Group f/64," *Camera Craft,* Vol. 42 (March 1935), pp. 107-8, 110.

Ehrens, Susan. "Interview with Alma Lavenson," *Photo Metro* (October 1986), pp. 13-20. Nineteen photographs reproduced.

———. "Alma Lavenson: A Ninetieth Birthday Retrospective," *re:view,* Newsletter of The Friends of Photography, Vol. 10, no. 5 (May 1987). Article on exhibition and excerpts from Ehrens interview with Lavenson, illustrated.

"Exposition, San Francisco's 164th Anniversary Is Celebrated on the Island," *San Francisco Chronicle* (June 30, 1940), p. 10.

"Faces Photographed," *Photo Metro* (January 1985), p. 21. Ex. rev., *San Ildefonso Indians.*

"The Family of Man," *The Sunday Times,* London (July 22, 1956), p. 1. Ex. announcement, *San Ildefonso Indians.*

"Focus on Europe and America," *U.S. Camera* (June 1950), pp. 37-52., *California Farm,* p. 40.

Fox, Louis William. "Alma Lavenson—The Spirit of Place," *Artweek,* Vol. 10, no. 7 (February 19, 1979), p. 11. Ex. rev., *Composition* (1931), *Stewart Store, French Corral* (1939), *Chichicastenango* (1959), *Glass Circles* (1931).

Frankenstein, Alfred. "Artist and Architect Meet in a Gallery," *San Francisco Chronicle* (November 12, 1939), *This World,* p. 17. Ex. rev.

———. "August Rodin's Exhibit Commemorates a Birthday," *San Francisco Chronicle* (November 17, 1940), *This World,* p. 13. Ex. rev.

———. "Just One Group Show after Another," *San Francisco Chronicle* (November 9, 1941), *This World,* p. 13. Ex. rev.

———. *San Francisco Chronicle* (June 14, 1942), *This World,* pp. 17. Ex. rev.

———. "The Women Artists Remember the War," *San Francisco Chronicle* (November 22, 1942), *This World,* p. 30. Ex. rev.

———. "In the Art World: Women's Show Runs True to Form," *San Francisco Chronicle* (November 11, 1946), p. 12. Ex. rev.

———. "The Camera Looks at Man—503 Vivid Studies," *San Francisco Chronicle, This World* (January 27, 1957), pp. 17-19. Ex. rev.

———. "Acquisitions at the De Young," *San Francisco Chronicle* (November 6, 1960), pp. 23-24. Ex. rev.

———. "Varied Show by Women Artists," *San Francisco Chronicle* (January 11, 1964), p. 27. Ex. rev. SFWA.

Fried, Alexander. "Bay Women Hold Annual Art Display," *San Francisco Examiner* (November 22, 1942), p. S-7. Ex. rev. SFWA.

Gage, Elizabeth. "Artist with a Camera," *Oakland Tribune* (October 29, 1967), p. 1-S. Feature article includes photograph of Lavenson.

Getlein, Frank. "In Paint and Film They Saw a Precise Image of America," *Smithsonian,* Vol. 13, no. 8 (November 1982), pp. 130-141. Ex. rev., *Tank, Union Oil Company* (1931).

Hagan, R. H. "Big Art Exhibits On For Holiday Season," *San Francisco Chronicle* (November 30, 1952), p. 29. Ex. rev. SFWA.

———. "Long Abstract Step by S.F. Women Artists," *San Francisco Chronicle* (November 21, 1956), p. 18. Ex. rev. SFWA.

Heyman, Therese. "California Scenes: A Sense of Past," *The Museum of California,* The Oakland Museum (April 1977).

"Honoring the Photographers," *Oakland Tribune* (March 11, 1968), p. 25. Photograph of Lavenson.

"Horse Show at Museum Fascinating," *San Francisco Chronicle* (November 27, 1932), p. D-3. Ex. rev. SFWA.

Humphrey, John. "The Henry Swift Collection of the San Francisco Museum of Art," *Camera,* no. 2 (February 1973), pp. 4, 13-14, 23. *San Ildefonso Indians,* p. 20.

"John O'Shea Holds Exhibition of Water Colors, Drawings and Oils at the Legion of Honor," *Oakland Tribune* (April 29, 1934), p. S-12. Ex. rev. of one-person show at 683 Brockhurst.

Kaplan, Sheila. "A Photographer Looks Back," *The Montclarion,* Montclair, California, (October 24, 1979), pp. 1, 5. Feature article and ex. rev. of retrospective.

Kennedy, Donna. "A 'Snapshooter' Solos at the University Gallery," *The Riverside Press-Examiner* (January 26, 1979), pp. E-1, E-2. Feature article and ex. rev. of retrospective.

Kieffer, Nancy. "Her Talent Comes to Light, Recognition Gaining on Photographer Alma Lavenson," *The Montclarion* (August 26, 1986), pp. 10-11. Feature article.

Lufkin, Liz. "Ranking with the Greats," *San Francisco Chronicle* (June 1, 1987), p. 53. Ex. rev., The Friends of Photography, *Self-Portrait* (1932).

Mann, Margery. "The Henry F. Swift Collection of Photographs by the f/64 Group, San Francisco Museum of Art," *Artforum* (November, 1963), p. 53. Ex. rev.

"Maurice Logan Leads Vote for Best Painting," *Oakland Tribune* (April 16, 1933), p. S-8.

Miller, Donald. "Praise a Continual Surprise for Photographer, 90," *Pittsburgh Post-Gazette* (June 20, 1987), p. 14. Feature article, *San Ildefonso Indians.*

Murray, Joan. "An Era Still Intact," *Artweek* (November 5, 1963), p. 11. Ex. rev., *Self-Portrait,* and *Sun Stones.*

———. "Two Photography Shows, Two Photography Books," *Westart* (March 20, 1970), p. 2. Ex. rev., *Ethiopian Girl.*

———. "Alma Lavenson—The Spirit of Place," *Artweek* (February 17, 1979), p. 110. Ex. rev., *Composition* (1933), *Chichicastenango* (1959), *Stewart Store, French Corral* (1939), *Glass Circles* (1931).

"Museum Opens Show of Lavenson Photos," *The Montclarion* (October 10, 1979), p. 6. Ex. rev.

"New Exhibits at de Young Park Museum," *San Francisco Chronicle* (August 21, 1932), p. D-3. Ex. rev.

"New Show to Open in S. F. Art Galleries," *Oakland Tribune* (April 2, 1933), p. S-8. Ex. rev.

Newhall, Beaumont. *"Image of Freedom," The Bulletin of the Museum of Modern Art,* 2, Vol. 9 (November 1941), p. 14.

"Notes," *Newsletter of the Friends of Photography,* 3, no. 1 (January 1980), p. 2.

Novakov, Anna. "Alma Lavenson at 90," *The Museum of California,* The Oakland Museum (May-June 1987), p. 18, 19. Feature article, *San Ildefonso Indians.*

"Oakland Art Annual Opens on March 4," *Oakland Tribune* (February 18, 1934), p. S-12.

Orr, Robin. "Two Celebrities Exhibit Art," *Oakland Tribune* (November 9, 1960), p. S-36. Ex rev.

"Piedmonter to Exhibit Photographs," *The Piedmonter,* Piedmont, California (May 13, 1981), p. 6. Ex. rev., *Doll in a Window* and *Balloon Inflating.*

"Photo Exhibit," *The Berkeley Voice* (October 19, 1983), p. 6. Ex. rev., *Embarcadero Center.*

"Photo Show at de Young Museum," *San Francisco Examiner* (August 14), p. 6-E.

"Photo Show at Museum," *The Piedmonter* (November 14), 1979, p. 5. Ex. rev., *Man with Sickle.*

"Photographer Alma Lavenson Dies at 92," *The Museum of California,* The Oakland Museum (November-December 1989), p. 27. Obituary.

"Photography," *Oakland Tribune* (March 27, 1966), p. 23-CM.

"Photography as Art," *The Boston Sunday Herald* (May 17, 1964), p. 36. Ex. rev., *Spiral, Tomar, Portugal* (1962).

"Photography Exhibit," *The Piedmonter* (October 19, 1983), p. 4. Ex. rev., *Embarcadero Center.*

"Photography Pioneers," *Oakland Tribune* (November 20, 1966), p. 24-CM. Ex. rev.

Porter, Allan. "Group f/64," *Camera,* no. 2 (February 1973), p. 3, 5-12, 15-22, 24-42.

"Pre-War Paris Shown in Pageant of Photography," *Oakland Tribune* (July 7, 1940), p. B-7.

"Prize Works in Women's Show Named," *San Francisco Examiner* (November 13, 1938), p. S-13.

San Francisco Chronicle (June 12, 1932), p. D-3. Ex. rev.

San Francisco Examiner (April 23, 1933), pp. 6-E. Ex. rev.

Sipes, Les. "Bay Area Well Respected in Photo—Fine Arts Exhibit," *Oakland Tribune* (January 3, 1965), pp. 11-CM. Ex. rev., *Spiral, Tomar, Portugal* (1962).

Stull, Christopher. "Etchings and Lithographs Come Out of Office," *San Francisco Chronicle* (November 3, 1940), *This World,* p. 19. Ex. rev. SFWA.

_____. "A Few Pictures Are Hung As Brass Is Polished," *San Francisco Chronicle* (November 10, 1940), *This World,* p. 17. Ex. rev. SFWA.

"Testaments of an Era," *San Francisco Chronicle and Examiner* (September 3, 1978), p. 7-9.

"Travel Salon Shows Photos at Museum; New Exhibits at de Young Park Museum," *San Francisco Chronicle* (August 21, 1932), p. D3.

"Two Approaches to Photography," *Westart,* Vol. 19, no. 17 (May 22, 1981), p. 1. Ex. rev., *Doll in a Window.*

"Visual Revolution Remains Strong After 46 Years," *West County Journal,* (April 12, 1978), p. 4D. Ex. rev.

Wessels, Glenn. "The Art Worlds," *The Argonaut* (February 16, 1934), p. 13. Ex. rev., *Mills College.*

Wolff, Pat. "The Inland Empire," *Westart* (January 26, 1979), p. 14., Ex. rev.

"Women Artists Hold S. F. Show," *Oakland Tribune* (November 19, 1933), p. 8-S. Ex. rev. SFWA.

Archival Collections

Alma Lavenson Wahrhaftig Family Collection
Papers and photographs from the personal collection of Alma Lavenson. Includes biographical and genealogical material: clippings, articles, correspondence, and photographs. Extensive folders of clippings and related materials about her father, Albert Lavenson. Material about her husband, Matt Wahrhaftig, including his unpublished article on the Mother Lode, dated 1947, and memoirs, dated 1934-1943. Includes extensive records of her photography career: notebooks, scrapbooks, correspondence, newspaper articles, exhibition announcements, and reviews.

Judah L. Magnes Museum, Berkeley, California, Western Jewish History Center
Archive Collection, Alma Lavenson Wahrhaftig Collection
Papers and photographs, 1855-1985, 30 items. Includes biographical and genealogical material, catalogs, announcements of her exhibitions, clippings; photographs of Lavenson, her husband, and her family. Information about her father and her grandparents.

Oral History Collection
Tapes and transcripts of *Interview with Alma Lavenson Wahrhaftig* conducted by Elinor Mandelson, September 25, 1978-April 21, 1980; An unpublished memoir by Matt Wahrhaftig, written April, 1935; family photographs and clippings with accompanying notes by Alma Lavenson.

Susan Ehrens Collection
Includes unpublished transcripts and tapes of interviews with Alma Lavenson conducted by Susan Ehrens, 1986.

Selected Collections

A single asterisk indicates a significant collection of more than ten of Alma Lavenson's photographs. Two asterisks denote a major collection of more than 300 photographs.

Public Collections

*The Baltimore Museum of Art, Baltimore, Maryland

**The Bancroft Library, University of California, Berkeley, California

The Brooklyn Museum, Brooklyn, New York

*California Museum of Photography, Riverside, California

Center for Creative Photography, Ansel Adams Collection, Tucson, Arizona

The Detroit Institute of Art, Detroit, Michigan

Fred Jones Jr. Memorial Art Center, University of Oklahoma Museum of Art, Norman, Oklahoma

Galleries of the Claremont Colleges, Claremont, California

J. Paul Getty Museum, Malibu, California

Judah L. Magnes Memorial Museum, Berkeley, California

The Metropolitan Museum of Art, New York, New York

Mills College Art Gallery, Oakland, California

The Museum of Fine Arts, Houston, Texas

The Museum of Modern Art, New York, New York

National Gallery of Art, Washington, D.C.

New Orleans Museum of Art, New Orleans, Louisiana

**The Oakland Museum, Oakland, California

Philadelphia Museum of Art, Philadelphia, Pennsylvania

*San Francisco Museum of Modern Art, San Francisco, California

Seattle Art Museum, Seattle, Washington

Stanford University Museum and Art Gallery, Stanford, California

University Art Museum, California State University, Long Beach, California

Corporate Collections

Consolidated Freightways, Inc., Menlo Park, California

Pacific Telesis Group, San Francisco, California

Alma Lavenson's photographs
are available through
Alma Lavenson Associates
P.O. Box 11426
Berkeley, CA 94704

Project Consultant: Leland Rice
Editor: Gail Larrick
Graphic Designer: Bruce Montgomery
Typographer: A.T. Composition
Printer: Gardner Lithograph
Bookbinder: Roswell Bookbinding
Typefaces: ITC Berkeley Oldstyle,
set on an Alphatype CRS
Text and Cover Papers: Centura Gloss